Shar's Story:

A Mother and Daughter Reunited

by

Sharon Shaw Elrod

Shar's Story:
A Mother and Daughter Reunited

Copyright 2005
by
Sharon Shaw Elrod
Cover Design by Joel D. Elrod

ISBN 1-932196-72-2

WordWright.biz
WordWright Business Park
46561 SH 118
Alpine, TX 79830

Printed in the United States of America

Praise for Shar's Story

This mother's love story began with the birth of her child who became a special gift to another family. The private agony of that decision haunted Sharon for over 35 years. Sharon brings to life her untold story and the journey to the reunion of a mother and daughter. I feel privileged to have shared these days with Sharon, as she and Katherine came to discover each other, build relationships and learned to love.

Doris Hayes
Author of *Against All Odds*

Dr. Sharon Shaw Elrod's successful professional career was immersed in child welfare, education and counseling with the goal of assisting children and adults better navigate the oftentimes rough terrain of everyday life. And yet it was not until Sharon recently dared to examine more intentionally a broken moment in her own young adulthood that she more fully experienced the deep joy of human and spiritual reconciliation and reunion! Her story is compelling when spoken, and now it is written, in anticipation that the shattered in the reader's life may be gathered and made whole.

Rev. Donald Strauch
Executive Director
Tucson Metropolitan Ministries/Family Services, Inc.

Sharon's journey is a common one, and her story will be uplifting to many readers. Her courage to share the truth and be available for her daughter to find her brought her much deserved relief. Birth parents carrying the guilt and shame of secrecy may find hope in Sharon's story and the courage to seek the support she found.

Marcie Velen, MSW, ACSW
Director, Permanency Planning
Arizona's Children Association

... a compelling story of a birthmother's unselfish love for her daughter and it's neverending power. This is a story anyone can appreciate, not just those involved in the adoption triad. It is a moving testimony to parenthood.

DeeAnn Barber, MSW, ACSW,
Chief Operating Officer
Arizona's Children Association

This book is dedicated to Jerry,

who never allowed the light of hope

to dim on the candle of my life.

All my love,

SASE

Acknowledgements

Many shared this journey with me and I am grateful to all. I thank my sisters, Jeannine, Marlene, and Pat, and my father, who know what unconditional love really is. To Aunt Dori, who provided love, encouragement, technical support and a lot of editing assistance!

Thanks to Phu and Desiree Thamithitikin for sharing so generously photographs they shot the weekend of my family's 2003 Shaw-Bang!

American Homefinding Association and its executive director, Tom Lazio, are the best in professional social work practice! I remain forever indebted to Tom and AHFA for keeping me reined in and for emotional support over 36 years.

Grateful loving appreciation to my son, Joel, who always wanted a sister, and whose artistic talents are so beautifully displayed on the cover of this book.

Deeply abiding and eternally grateful thanks go to Jerry, one love, one lifetime.

And to Katherine, without whose courage and curiosity, the story would not have been possible, and the secret place in my heart—now full of joy and happiness—would still have been empty.

Shar's Story:
Mother and Daughter Reunited

When do stories begin? Perhaps none really begin, but only emerge gradually with pieces of the story coming together at different times, over many years. This story began to take shape in early January 2002, with seeds planted many years before Baby arrived. The individual stories along the way somehow end up making the whole, making sense of the journey. This human story tries to make sense out of the chaos and pathos and joy of a journey.

Chapter 1

July 2002
This Message is for Sharon

I find gardening and music therapeutic. The garden needed tending that hot East Texas summer day in July 2002. The weeds, clumped so thick they shrouded the tomatoes and beans in thick prickly stems, difficult to pull up from the dry hard ground. July in the Piney Woods never varies from hot and dry. Never enough rain to suit even the locals, who whined about the summer, but never considered living anywhere else in the world.

I had a wet towel around my neck, trying to keep the rest of me from getting too hot. As we built our retirement home during the summer of 1998, I discovered the wet towel kept the rest of my body from burning up. I needed to get the weeding done, and needed the help the wet towel offered. Just another few minutes and I'd break for lunch in an air-conditioned house.

Jerry sauntered through the gate and called to me, "Time for lunch, sweetheart. Give it up for a few minutes." With relief, I put the weeding fork down and headed into the kitchen to make sandwiches. After an hour heating up on the sidewalk, the gallon jug of sun tea was more than ready. Too strong, it needed lots of ice and some water.

As I pulled the bread out of the drawer and headed around the kitchen island to get a knife, Jerry said, "Here's a message on the phone..." and pushed the play button.

The voice said, "This message is for Sharon. This is Tom Lazio from American Homefinding in Ottumwa, Iowa; your daughter called me and she wants to make contact with you."

My memory of that moment forward is forever set in stone. I can recall every minute, what I did and said, and what others said to me. I stared with disbelief at the telephone, tears starting to well up in my eyes. I stood locked in place on the far side of the island. I said, "Oh my God!" Jerry began laughing and crying all at the same time.

"Oh, honey!" He came to me as I lost my balance, encircled me with his big strong arms, and together we slowly lowered ourselves to the floor. We sat together laughing and crying for several minutes.

Tom's message said to call him as soon as I got the message; it was Friday and he wanted to leave the office for the day.

I called Tom immediately. We had talked several times over 36 years. He knew how deeply I desired to reunite with Rachael Ann. He had called her on my behalf when she turned 21; he told her then that, should she choose to do so, she could make contact with me. His report to me 15 years ago said that she thought she'd like to do that someday. But I had never heard from her. Until today.

Tom waited for my call. I started to speak and my voice cracked. He said, "I know how emotional this is for you, Sharon! You have waited such a long time for this day!"

"It's so hard to believe! Tell me everything you can!"

I retired from social work, managed adoption and foster care programs, and worked with clients in private and public agencies for years; confidentiality remains a cornerstone of my profession, and I knew those important rules also bound him.

"Your daughter called me this morning and said she'd decided it was time she contact you," Tom reported. I could tell he chose his words very carefully.

"I suggested to her that she write an email and I'll forward it on to you." Tom wasn't telling me anything about Baby. He said only that she had decided to open the door.

"She agreed to send an email, saying she'd write it today. I'll forward it on to you as soon as I get it." And then he repeated his mantra of more than 30 years, "Timing is everything!"

My head agreed but my heart leapt with impatient joy.

I'd waited fifteen years for this day, and hoped for over thirty-six years. Thirty-six years! Such a long time ago, and such a different socio-cultural experience back then. The Cultural Revolution that women brought to the last two decades of the century had reached only its infancy in 1966. The small box with well-defined boundaries still trapped women in the space in which they'd live out their lives. Their mothers usually constructed these boxes. While men traditionally defined female roles, women blindly accepted their handiwork and perpetuated it in the socially accepted milieu. Like racism, exposed in the previous decade, feminism in small town Iowa amounted to marrying and giving birth, and getting a teaching degree in the event of early widowhood. Women in 1966 only began to wonder about how their roles might change. They'd not yet found the courage to change.

In December 1965, we made preparations for sister Marlene's wedding on the 26th of December. Just two years older, I stood as her Maid of Honor, and frantically tried to get through the event without anyone finding out about my pregnancy. Although I almost fainted during the wedding, I made an excuse about feeling overheated in the taffeta gown and fur muff. No one suspected my condition. I hadn't had the nerve to tell anyone yet.

Because I could not bear to see my parents' disappointment, my older sister, Jeannine, agreed to tell Mom and Dad about my pregnancy. The culture of the time also determined their response: "I hope you do something to straighten yourself out." At the time, they blamed me and offered no emotional support or understanding. (After experiencing the opportunity to grow beyond 1960's social expectations, Mom and Dad ultimately became reassuring and loving about my single parenting experience.)

I called the bio-father of my unborn child. I don't know if he responded automatically or if he just didn't want to have anything to do with me. He told me there wasn't anything he could do about it. Our summer romance left me feeling more connected with him than he with me. He left Iowa for his home in another state, and I never spoke with him again.

I remember saying aloud after I hung up the telephone, "Well, Baby, it's just you and me."

I don't know when I ever felt so alone. I just wanted

someone to care, someone to hold my hand. But Baby and I faced this alone, and Baby only kicked, a feeble little flutter that let me know she heard me.

The Episcopal priest and his wife at my church, found American Homefinding Association in Ottumwa, Iowa. They said I could go there and wait for Baby's birth in secret. I needn't tell anyone. I could hide. There, too, Baby and I faced this alone.

Chapter 2

January 1966
Baby and Me—Alone

I just disappeared. Baby and I arrived in Ottumwa on a cold winter day in January 1966. Throughout the next five months, I saw no one that I knew, except my parents. My mother came to see me after a couple of months. And both of them came to see me the weekend before Baby arrived. My younger sister, Pat, sent me a Mother's Day card, the only one I received. It touched me so much I sobbed for a long time that day.

I spent my days sewing and learning to knit. I made a pink sweater-top kind of thing, never wore it, and never knitted another thing again in my life. I never watched soap operas, probably because I finished college (my scripted teaching degree) at 21 and immediately went to work. Now going on 23, pregnant and not married, I needed to keep my mind occupied so I watched soap operas.

The staff treated me with kindness and caring. Because I was an older unwed mother, Alan Seabrook, the director of the agency, decided to counsel me himself. With skill and insight, he wove a path through my defenses and false bravado, "I'm fine. I can handle this. I'll get through it."

I wasn't fine. I fumbled through the emotional trauma facing me, and stumbled from one day to the next.

Alan gently insisted on talking. We talked about how alone I felt and about what contributed to the lack of support from my family (in addition to the socio-cultural influences).

My parents found me a difficult child to rear, primarily because I resisted others' control. The child-rearing game plan of the 1940s and 1950s in small-town Iowa consisted of controlling and managing children's behavior because, after all, their behavior reflected the value and worth of the parents. Mother proudly reported to us numerous times during our childhood years that she had made a deal with God: God gave her healthy children and she kept liquor out of the house. She got her healthy children, four pretty little girls. She and Daddy managed our behavior well, mostly with lots of love, frowns when we disobeyed and long detailed explanations about why we should behave as they thought best.

Children do not consciously plan to behave in certain ways, but I know somewhere deep inside I felt a strong need to control my life and not turn it over to my parents, even at the tender age of three or four. I turned obstinate and stubborn.

I always found special joy in music. Number one sister, Jeannine, began taking piano lessons in kindergarten. Even at that young age, she showed great ability to read music and play piano, according to reports of adults who listened to her play. Mother never said why, but she placed me in piano lessons also; I suspect she wanted to get me out of her hair. Or more likely, I probably badgered her to do the same thing my big sister did. Whatever her reasoning, I began taking piano lessons at age four.

I loved listening to the radio. A family story reveals the source of my nickname, Jo. I walked and talked prior to the age of one; one evening while Daddy dressed in an upstairs dressing closet, I began a half-crawl, half-walk up the flight of thirteen steps.

He heard me and cried out, "Who's coming up the steps?"

I replied with something I had heard on the radio that day, "Jo Jo!" The name stuck.

I soon discovered, after beginning the piano lessons, that I preferred to play what I heard on the radio rather than practice my lesson. This started some of the tension between Mother and me, an ever-present tension that arose between two very similar personalities.

Raising a strong-willed child never presents an easy task for any parent, and it's more difficult when the parent is also strong-willed. Parent-child clashes grow both inevitable and numerous; they only vary in intensity and duration.

In another family story, Mother attempted to help all four of her daughters with their penmanship by installing a chalkboard on the wall in the kitchen. She drew lines on it and instructed us to practice writing within the lines and with identical slants on each letter. When predictably I refused to comply, Mother attempted to hold my hand to show me how to stay within the lines.

I jerked my hand away and cried, "Do my lone!"

My penmanship today reflects the lack of discipline Mother tried so hard to instill in me.

The pattern of dissension between us built, one experience upon another, throughout my childhood. Mother tried to shape and guide my life, while I refused her efforts at shaping and guidance. Daddy told me in my adult life that he thought Mother knew how to parent better, so he always deferred to her.

I suppose it's not too surprising that, when faced with a pregnancy that fell outside lines of social acceptability, my parents possessed neither knowledge nor resources to help me. My pregnancy shocked them so badly they did not know what to say or do. So on my own I made all the arrangements for disappearing until after Baby's birth. I told Mom and Dad what I had decided, then left.

My counselor helped me to see that blaming myself for my pregnancy neither helped nor made sense. He showed me that blame did not produce good results. Planning how to change my life and control my future helped much more. He showed me how to concentrate on that planning and I love him to this day for that help. He helped me see that although my parents had flaws, I could and would love them anyway. He also helped me see that my profession didn't fit me. I had always followed the wrong script.

I knew little about social work. I began to read some of his library and discovered a kinship with the work described. Alan called a close friend, the dean of the School of Social Work in Lincoln, Nebraska. Enrollment for the fall of 1966 continued, and there were a couple of openings. I applied and the school accepted me into the masters degree program. What a thrill! I had done it with help from Alan, but otherwise on my own, and it felt entirely different from anything I had ever done before. I now wonder how reading about law or politics or medicine or veterinary medicine or any number of other professions now available to young women might've changed my life.

Before her birth, Baby and I spent time walking and reading the last couple of months. She moved a lot and loved to exercise while I walked or tried to sleep. I soon discovered that she loved hearing me sing. So when she started kicking and moving her arms, I sang to her. She then kicked and flung her arms about more slowly, and sometimes in rhythm to my voice. At night, soon after I started to sing to her, she'd fall asleep and sleep very soundly until early morning.

On the morning of May 31, a Tuesday, I awoke with my back aching like crazy. When I got out of bed, I felt strange. Not only did my back hurt, but my stomach muscles moved in spasms. I was in labor. I timed the contractions for almost an hour, and when they shortened to about five minutes apart, I went downstairs to tell Mrs. Green. She was irritated that I hadn't told her immediately, but then the labor pains stopped. So we didn't rush to the hospital. We waited until early afternoon, when they got close together again, and she took me to the hospital.

That starting and stopping routine continued for 36 hours. I was alone, of course. My counselor came to see me a couple of times; another social worker came. They treated me very kindly, but I was alone.

An order of Roman Catholic nuns, well-trained nurses, managed the hospital. Attentive to my condition and ready to assist, they checked on me regularly and insisted I keep walking to keep labor progressing. I didn't want to walk, but they insisted. So I walked the halls…alone.

The nurses lacked training as caring human beings. I experienced their attitude as punitive. They came into my room and gave orders; I felt as if I should salute and respond, "Yes, Ma'am." They explained nothing to me about their actions or why they needed to do what they did. Childbirth almost feels tolerable when the mother knows what's happening. When she knows little, when no one tells her anything and treats her with uncaring hands and disdain, childbirth turns into a frightening experience. I felt fear, and terribly alone.

I believe that Baby just wasn't ready to leave me yet, so she took her time, as did my body in responding to her. I also believe she was angry with me because she knew my plans, and she delayed her birth in her tiny attempt to fend off the inevitable.

On the evening of the second day in the hospital, the physician partner of my obstetrician came into my labor room and announced, "Your doctor is out of town and I have to deliver you."

I dreaded this possibility. Alan had told me he hoped my doctor would be available for delivery because the partner, although competent, had a poor bedside manner and Alan did not have good feedback about him from other birth mothers. He reportedly treated unwed mothers punitively and roughly.

Indeed, he proved rough in handling my exhausted and sore body and seemed to enjoy creating more pain for me. After examining me, he pronounced with obvious delight, "You're not going to deliver this one on your own; I'll have to get it started." I did not know what that meant, but my fear escalated dramatically. I'd felt considerable pain and discomfort for two full days and one night, had not slept or eaten, (I frankly did not want to eat), and he was going to start something that he did not explain to me.

I soon learned what his "getting it started" comment meant. He manually cut the embryonic sac and water gushed out on the labor cot. He reported triumphantly, "There! That should do it!" He seemed proud of his feat.

The nuns did not clean up the water forced from my body. I lay there on soaked sheets and the final stages of labor began with a vengeance. I wept, not from the pain, but from the coldness I felt to the depths of my soul. *I was so alone.*

I gave birth shortly before midnight on Wednesday, June 1. Baby weighed in at exactly my birth weight and length. Fat and beautiful, she had black hair like mine. She was perfect. Then I went into shock, shivering uncontrollably. The nuns brought me a blanket, but I couldn't stop shivering. I wept and shivered, and remained alone.

Two days later Alan came to see me with the relinquishment papers. He repeated what he had said several times in the previous months, that they could keep her in foster care for a while in case I wanted to delay signing the papers; but that wasn't my plan. He told me the staff had identified adoptive parents, educated, caring people and that he thought they'd make wonderful parents. I made up my mind that she was going to go to them, and I told her she had to come back and find me someday. I numbed my senses to prepare for the inevitable. I named her Rachael Ann on her original birth certificate. I signed the papers, left the hospital, and returned to civilization.

Chapter 3

1966-2002
Life After Baby

I found graduate school fun and challenging. I'd always breezed through academics. My masters degree was no exception. But I had more important experiences with friends and learned to relate again to men after having Baby. Terrified of becoming pregnant again, I behaved for a while like a prudish virgin insistent upon protecting myself. I felt reluctant even to kiss a man.

When a relationship with a graduate student in another field turned semi-serious, I allowed my defenses to relax and for the first time in my life, had a happy and healthy relationship with a man. My determination to complete my bachelors degree as quickly as possible did not allow much time for socializing and dating during those years. What a stupid choice!

But that differed from my time in graduate school in Lincoln, and the change felt great. I got a masters degree in social work and enjoyed life at the same time.

Jon and I dated for about a year, spending time together in the summer visiting my parents, and seeing each other several times a week during the school year. At the end of that summer, Jon left graduate school and moved to Kansas City to take a corporate job. Eager to start making money, he decided he did not need the graduate degree. I made several trips to see him, and the last one included several friends who went along to attend a conference there.

Toward the end of that weekend, I walked in on Jon and my best friend in an embrace in his bedroom. The hurt was almost more than I could bear at the time. But within a few days, I reminded myself of Baby, and how letting go of *her* felt. The other pain paled by comparison. I had experienced the greatest loss possible in my life; anything after Baby I could manage with relative ease.

⚃ ⚃ ⚃

I moved to Omaha when I finished graduate school in Lincoln. In the second year of my masters degree program, I finished my field experience in Omaha at a community center in an African American neighborhood. I'd never worked with families in incredibly impoverished living conditions. I found in myself an innate compassion for people victimized by political maneuverings and social stratification. Many people in my social circle took the easy way and blamed the victims. After spending three years working with them, I found no justification for blaming them for their plight. My views about that have never changed.

My move to Omaha came with a new experience in dating, one that I had only just begun. At 25, I knew I was a novice. So I decided to give myself as much variety as I could, and my real dating life began in earnest!

I discovered I was as good a companion at a ball game as watching a movie. If I found something in a man that I did not like, or a viewpoint or value I disagreed with, I simply stopped seeing him. I dismissed all the notions I had acquired earlier in my life about pleasing men at my own expense. I'd mastered the "be nice" behavior at an early age. Now I learned how to stand up for myself.

By the time I turned 30, all three of my sisters were married and having babies. My family never asked, but I have no doubt they wondered if I'd ever marry.

My career as an educator on the university level began in 1970 when I accepted a position at the University of Nebraska Medical Center. I began working as a psychiatric social worker on the children's unit of the separate psychiatric hospital. A whole new part of my life opened up when I made that change.

I discovered another natural interest of mine, counseling and psychotherapy with individuals and couples with relationship problems. Over the years that interest led me to establishing a private practice in Omaha, one of the pioneer practices for social workers in that city. I also developed an interest in women's issues and worked with a number of leaders of feminism in the early years of that movement. I treasure an award from the Omaha Women's Political Caucus for Outstanding Community Service to the people and city of Omaha.

I celebrated a full and good life! I had an excellent position at the University Medical Center, after a promotion to director of Social Services in 1973. I dated many different men and enjoyed the variety. I did not seriously consider settling down to just one, and certainly not marriage. I bought a home of my own during those years and felt very comfortable with my life. I enjoyed traveling, which I did a lot.

A friend from my early days in Omaha presided over one of the volunteer boards on which I held a committee chairperson position. Jerry Elrod and I met when I first worked for the community center and he served on the board of directors. In September 1967, my field experience had just begun. The board met late that afternoon; I sat at my desk.

As I looked up, I saw him walk by the door, turn around and look into my office and say, "Well, what have we here!"

I introduced myself and we chatted briefly. That began a friendship that lasted forever.

Jerry was married with a child on the way. My friendship with him included his wife, also named Jerry, and their son, Joel. We all had a lot in common, including our dedication to righting social wrongs and working for significant change in the lives of people victimized socially and politically. We also traveled in the same circles socially.

Lots of people knew Jerry in Omaha and throughout the United Methodist Church. As a clergyman, he spoke for the church on social issues of the time, and the Omaha World Herald often quoted him. People considered him a community leader, and honored and respected him for his skills and leadership.

By the time Jerry and I served together on the Douglas County Mental Health Association Board, we had worked together on a variety of issues and shared many social times. His marriage had ended and women sought after him. He was bright, witty, funny, a great companion, and very sexy!

I'd resisted dating him for four years after his divorce because of my friendship with his former wife. Clearly we were attracted to each other, but I established firm boundaries, and kept them in place. However, in July 1974 I decided to loosen the boundaries and asked him to have dinner at my home to talk about some mental health board issues.

It had been a tough day. My office handled central admissions, which meant social workers in my office initially interviewed all adult psychiatric patients, and then referred them to the appropriate clinic in the hospital. Admissions came in all day that day.

I got home as Jerry pulled up to the curb in front of the house. He knew immediately that I had no dinner prepared, much less started. His sensitivity pushed through, and he suggested, "Let's go out for dinner."

"That's a great idea," I responded. Having thought about this on the drive home, I added, "Where would you like to go?"

Ever so thoughtful, Jerry said, "Wherever you want."

"How about the Café de Paris?" I knew the upscale French restaurant as one of many great eating establishments in Omaha. He had no intention of going to a place that pricey, I feel sure, but he agreed without hesitation. I hid my ulterior motives, but I definitely had a plan!

We talked very little about mental health issues and a

lot about ourselves and what paths our lives had taken since his divorce. Because of my boundary issues, we'd spent little time together since then. At the end of the evening, I told him I wanted to spend more time with him. I confessed I was in love with him and that I wanted to see where our relationship would go if we agreed to date.

Jerry was dumbfounded! We both felt the mutual attraction, but I had never told him how I felt about him. The next day I'd leave for a week with my family in Iowa, but we made plans to see each other upon my return. He was in a relationship with another woman at the time, and I knew he had some potential complications to deal with.

In mid-July, we began seeing each other regularly. And we discovered our friendship had indeed grown from fondness to love. As his former wife experienced problems of her own, he wanted to move Joel back to Omaha to live with him. That happened by early November. Then our relationship turned into a more family oriented one, and we spent a lot of time doing things that included Joel.

We talked about marriage off and on. He feared another marriage and another failure. I thought I wanted to marry, but wasn't altogether certain. So we just talked about it. Until March 1975.

I went to Arizona again that year with Mom and Dad. I had enjoyed vacationing with them there for several years. The experience allowed us to get away and spend time alone together, and they always seemed to enjoy having me visit them during their winter holiday in Phoenix.

Jerry made his decision while I spent the holiday in Arizona. He called and asked me to come home, that he wanted to talk about getting married. I had confided in

Mom and Dad about our yes-no talks about marriage. When I told them Jerry wanted me to return to Omaha because he wanted to make wedding plans, Mom said, "Well, he'd better mean it this time!" A protective mother hen, she watched over her last unmarried chick!

I flew back to Omaha, and Jerry asked me to marry him. I said yes.

I told him what Mom had said, and he called them in Phoenix and asked them to return home via Omaha so he could talk with them. When they arrived, Jerry asked them for permission to marry me. That was all Mom and Dad needed to hear.

We married on August 31, 1975, in the back yard of a beautiful home we bought. Joel participated in the ceremony, and we began a marriage and a family that turned into the stable center of each of our lives. It remains so today.

Jerry and Joel both knew about Baby. Joel wanted me to go get her so he could have a sister. At the tender age of seven, he did not understand the impossibility of this. Jerry began telling me then that he believed someday we'd hear from her. I always acknowledged his belief, but I did not allow myself to believe or hope with him. I had already lost her once, and if I allowed myself to hope and I never heard from her, I felt I'd lose her a second time. I did not believe I could live through that again.

Chapter 4

Jerry and I waited for the email from Rachael Ann. We still did not know her name, so we called her Rachael Ann. Everyone has a secret place in their heart where the dearest memories and feelings reside. A place where we put what we want to keep safest in our lives. In that place in my heart, Rachael Ann was always Baby. No matter what happened ever in the world, from prehistoric time to eternity, she'd stay my Baby. I gave birth to her and nothing in the world would ever change that. Not even the paper I signed to allow someone that I did not know to rear her. In retrospect, I cannot now imagine ever having done that. But time has a way of warping the stark reality of distant experiences, and the fact remains that the now-sealed document relinquishing all rights to Baby bears my name.

July 12 arrived. I couldn't wait to tell my family. And I felt so grateful for the privilege of telling them. While we waited for Baby's email, I sent this one to my family and closest friends:

Subj:Happy News
Date:7/12/02 12:46:21 PM Central Daylight Time

Hope you are all sitting down to read this...

I just rec'd a phone call that is changing our lives. My daughter who was born June 1, 1966, and whom I relinquished for adoption, has told the agency in Iowa that she is ready to become acquainted with me. I had given them permission about 15 years ago to give her my name/address should she ever inquire. And now I sit here waiting for an email that she sent the agency...

I'm in a surreal state and Jerry is napping. So I guess the world is still in place. I am so grateful that I shared this information with my Iowa family last January (aunts & cousins). Now I am able to include you in my happy news...

I kept the computer on all afternoon, checking it every few minutes. Close to midnight, I finally decided to try to sleep, knowing it would be almost impossible.

So I began to think back over the past six months. I didn't plan the trip to Iowa in January, either in context or experience. The dawning of realization about connections in life happens so slowly. But the dawning started that night as I awaited Baby's email. As an adult I have had to separate the many good experiences and lessons my parents provided from the few difficult and negative patterns and events. I believe a healthy adult can do this, and I, in my more mature years, try to measure my behavior against healthy yardsticks.

Thus, in spite of the negative influences from Mother's

attempts to over-manage a willful child, the positive aspects of our relationship always carried more weight. I loved my parents, and I will always know they loved me.

Mom provided me the opportunity, after years of piano lessons, to take organ lessons during the eighth year. She drove me to weekly lessons on an old tracker organ at a small college ten miles from our home. I fell in love with the instrument and the spectacular music it made. The keys are attached by "tracks" to the pipes in a huge box behind the organ, and as one plays the keys, the tracks open the pipes, allowing air to pass through and make the appropriate sound—thus the "tracker" label.

In my junior year of high school, I filled in for Jeannine playing the organ for church on Sunday mornings, when she needed a day off. I started as church organist in my senior year, beginning a long volunteer career of providing sacred music for worship in a variety of churches and settings.

So I had recently begun playing a tracker organ for the second time in my life. Following our retirement, Jerry and I attempted to find a United Methodist church in the Deep South, one similar in theology to that which experienced throughout our lives as United Methodists.

Soon after I transferred my membership to the local Episcopal church, the organist abruptly quit and we spent two Sundays without music in church. Becoming perturbed with the lack of music, I volunteered to "fill in," and this turned into a permanent solution. I enjoyed playing the tracker organ again, and every Sunday I played my favorites, Bach, Beethoven, Chopin and Baroque organ music written for the tracker.

The priest had a phenomenal gift for preaching and teaching without sounding preachy. The message I heard in church every Sunday morning for over a year was, "...live life authentically; be honest, kind, loving, full of mercy and kindness...stop lying to yourself and others...you are never going to be perfect, so get with it! Admit it! Accept your sins, your warts, your life-impacting mistakes, and work for change, to live better. Forgiveness and acceptance wait just around the corner, but you have to turn around the corner"

Memory sometimes plays tricks on us. I have no conscious memory of a plan, but the unfolding of the story occurred in such a strange way. And one of the connections fell into place, as I waited for sleep.

Chapter 5

January 2002
A Trip to Iowa

Aunt Pat and Aunt Fran, two of my mother's six sisters, had kept me posted on my favorite uncle's terminal condition. In January 2002 I got an email that indicated his earthly journey was coming to an end. Within minutes, I decided to drive to Iowa (1000 miles!) to say goodbye to him and see my extended family. I quickly put together plans for where I'd stay each day/night and confirmed the plans with each relative; there wasn't a glitch anywhere.

As I drove off, Jerry reminded me to keep the cell phone on. Three miles from home, the phone rang; I had left my vitamins and supplements on the kitchen counter, and he knew how they kept me feeling well; so I returned, found him at the gate with the forgotten items, got another loving hug and sped on my way.

Aunt Fran in Hiawatha, Iowa, hugged me next, when I arrived late the following night after a stopover with friends in Oklahoma City.

I don't remember making any conscious decision. I'd struggled with the dawning realization that my parents loved me throughout my life, but my mother didn't *like* me, or at least didn't like parts of me that I thought important to me. I'd started to admit the reality of our relationship, and the reality that my mother, although loving and caring, also controlled my sisters and me. The rebellion I exhibited was textbook: I'll show you that I will do what I want, when I want and how I want! Unfortunately, Mother never mastered the skill of communication with a child so similar in personality. Rebellion led to more attempts to control, which led to more rebellion. And as an adult, I became as controlling as my mother.

I'd talked with my Aunt Fran about all this on email; she listened caringly and responded with so much love it astounded me! I had to talk with Aunt Fran, as much as I had to say good-bye to Uncle Oliver.

During the marathon night of talking with Aunt Fran, I began to move toward the topic of my rebellious behavior…and finally, I plunged, "Did you know I had a child?"

Aunt Fran gave no visible reaction…just, "No." I felt immeasurable disbelief. "You mean Mother never told you about my baby girl?"

"No."

And so I told her about Baby. Born on June 1, 1966, same day that my sister Jeannine gave birth to Ann, and within two ounces and two hours of each other. And for the first time, it occurred to me that Mother had never revealed that she had an imperfect daughter who had given birth to a perfect baby.

As I began to discuss the experience with Aunt Fran, the picture developed. Mother had to preserve her own image as the perfect mother she projected to the world; thus she had to present her daughters as perfect. My pregnancy marred the perfect daughter image so she could not tell anyone about it. Mother was as much a victim of social expectations as I.

I do remember the moment I decided to change the way I lived. I made a determined choice to stop living a lie. I loved Baby with all my heart. I gave birth to her. And I gave her to loving people to adopt and raise as their own. I decided, sitting in Aunt Fran's living room, that I'd tell no more lies. Authentic life, *here I come!*

I told Aunt Fran of my plan to blow all the lies out of the water and tell the whole family that I had had Baby. A part of me regretted ever having signed those papers. I did it for cultural and familial reasons. I bought into the perfect daughter image. Perfect daughters don't have babies before they marry. And I had no social or family support or encouragement to think differently.

I treasure the time with Aunt Fran. I will remember it always. It ended too quickly, for me at least. I'm sure she didn't relish any more midnight marathons!

I went on to Cedar Falls to see Uncle Oliver and my Larkin relatives. The final journey of their father's life occupied their attention, and the timing didn't permit me to talk about Baby, who would turn 36 in a few months. We shared some wonderful times together; I talked with my uncle who still claimed (on his deathbed!) that he had saved my life when I, as a baby, almost rolled off his kitchen table. He grabbed my diapers and pulled me into his arms before I could fall! He loved that story, and I will treasure it always. I wish he'd known about Baby. I left his hospital bed that day with silent tears for the cruel experience fate delivers; the time had passed for telling one of my favorite human beings about Baby.

I lived with Cousin Dawn and her husband and family in my second year of college. I stayed with her during my time in Cedar Falls and thought her so special. Les, her husband, had died a couple of years before my visit and her grown children lived elsewhere. So we had a slumber party that extended over several nights! In those nights of talking into the wee hours, I learned that she had not known about Baby. She wanted to hear all the details. So I told her of my experience, including my 36 hours of labor in solitude with no family present, a punitive physician, and Catholic nurses who had too much to do to attend to an "…unwed mother…" delivering "…an illegitimate baby…" With tears in her eyes, Dawn said. "…if I had known, I would have been there with you." And I know she meant every word. I began to feel doors opening in my life, doors closed for 36 years. My dear family met Baby for the first time, and no one scolded or shook their fingers at us or told us we fell short of the acceptable. They loved and accepted us, not only in spite of who we were, but also because of it. My spirit soared!

Next I visited Aunt Pat. And we had lots to talk about. Each visit with relatives included my acceptance of the fact that my mother did not like me, but she did love me. Each visit included my new understanding of my mother's controlling behavior and the effect it had on me. Each relative shared with me experiences they had had with my mother that confirmed her controlling behavior, her need to be right and perfect and to have all the answers, and our love for her in spite of all the problems and issues. Each time I listened to their experiences, I felt an awareness of how much I'd turned into someone just like my mother. I disliked what I saw in myself.

Aunt Pat, also, did not know about Baby. She expressed what Aunt Fran and Dawn had already said, "We love you just the way you are...warts and all!" Aunt Pat added, "I always knew you weren't perfect!" What a relief! I wasn't perfect, and my family still loved me.

I left Iowa and drove back home to Texas in one long day. Uncle Oliver knew I'd come and gone. He died that morning, while I drove back to the Piney Woods.

I needed time to process my trip. I saw change on the horizon. I knew my life had become more authentic. I knew I'd never again lie or withhold information about Baby. I knew I'd accept her openly as part of my life, and never again pretend she did not exist. I'd admit my imperfections and never again retreat to lies and secrets. I'd learn to say I'm wrong, admit my mistakes. I'd relinquish control, listen more, and talk less. I'd turn into the good and loving person I envisioned. I felt wonderful as I started a new life!

Chapter 6

July 2002
Timing is Everything!

Saturday morning I stumbled to the computer before daybreak. Still no message. I began preparing myself again for living without Baby. Like the three or four days following her birth, I talked to myself most of the time. Life is not and never will be fair. You cannot undo what you have done when you sign irrevocable papers that relinquish all rights forever and ever, *Amen!* I tried to stay optimistic on the outside, but on the inside I felt growing despair. Two days of despair felt even worse.

Then late Sunday evening this email came from Tom:

Date:7/14/02 5:27:27 PM Central Daylight Time
Dear Sharon,

I know that you have waited a long time for this call! Glad that you called right back.

I've attached a note from your daughter that is self-explanatory. As soon as I hear from her again I will get

back in touch with you.
Timing is everything!

Peace and Joy,
Tom Lazio

I had to prepare myself to read the message from Baby.
So, with pure logic and unquestionable reason prevailing, I
screamed for Jerry and he came running.

I'm not quite sure how to start this letter — it's an
incredibly surreal experience! I guess the most important
thing to say is that I have a truly blessed life! I've been
married for almost 12 years to a generous, loving,
supportive man and we have 2 children. Our son is 9 years
old, handsome, athletic, and amazingly 'in touch' for
someone his age. Our daughter is 7 and extremely
intelligent; her ability to focus is phenomenal. I have
several pets, including dogs, cats, and horses (my friends
call me Mother Nature)! I have several true friends; women
I can always count on. My parents stay involved with the
kids and with our lives, even though we don't live near
each other now — we visit several times a year. I have one
brother; he's 16 months younger than I am. I enjoy music
and reading, and I love to spend any spare time at the lake.
Before the kids were born, I worked as a chemist for a
pharmaceutical lab. Now, I volunteer for the PTO and
serve on my state Hunter/Jumper Association Board of
Directors. School was always fun and easy for me — I had
the highest GPA in my high school graduating class and
graduated from college with high honors. I've always

thought of my intelligence as a gift; something wonderful that I didn't have to work hard for! I'm 5'8", blue eyes, brown hair (although it's blond now!), slim, and athletic (wow, I sound like an ad in the Personals). So why do I feel compelled to make this connection at this point? I've never felt anything was missing in my life; on the contrary, my parents helped me believe that I was special because I was chosen. However, my best friend has recently been involved in a life-threatening accident, and it made me realize that some opportunities must be seized before it's too late. I've always been comforted believing that there's somebody in the world that I don't know who loves me, and I guess I want my birth mother (and anyone else involved) to know that I am happy and blessed, and I know that my life is unfolding exactly as it should be.

All the years of wondering ended there. No one could measure my excitement, not even on the Richter scale! I'd no longer wake in the middle of the night and wonder if she knew I always loved her, wonder where she lived, what she was doing, if she had good and dependable friends, if she married, if she had children, the color of her eyes and hair, if she looked like me. Most important, I'd no longer have to wonder if she inherited my good brain. I never took credit for my intellect; I just got lucky and inherited good gray matter. And I hoped she got lucky too. She was happy! She had a good and loving family! She enjoyed the same things I did, and she had a great brain! I could not describe my excitement!

With my heart pounding and skipping beats, and my fingers trembling on the keyboard, I sat down at the computer to write my reply, and it sounded so trite. So I deleted the whole thing and started over; I repaired the second try three times before deleting that one, too. The third attempt ended up nine and a half pages long. Delete. After that I stopped counting. Finally, in frustration, I decided to respond to her with the same kind of information that she shared with me. I wanted to tell her all about my life and my family. And somehow I knew that I had to take it easy with the first baby steps in our reunion. I didn't want to scare her off with my first attempts to communicate, but I wanted her to know the important role she's played in my life. So I decided to send this to Tom to send on to Baby.

Subj:from Sharon
Date:7/14/02 6:56:23 PM Central Daylight Time

...and I am not sure how to start my response. So far I've reworked the first sentence 17 times, and deleted everything at least 25 times. So here goes...

The Executive Director at American Homefinding assured me over the years that you were with wonderful parents who loved you unconditionally, as they did their son. He also told me they were very bright people and would be sure you had all of life's opportunities that they could make available. Tom Lazio has also been helpful in providing appropriate information since his arrival at AM-Homefinding. Your letter confirms all that, and what a celebration it is to hear you describe it!

Life has been very good to me. I grew up in New

Hartford (Iowa) with three sisters who are still my best friends; Mom was a homemaker and Dad owned the local grain elevator. I graduated top in my high school class, and had honors in the remainder of my graduate programs—masters degree in social work and two doctorate programs in education and management of human services programs. I am 59 next Friday and I would still be taking classes somewhere if I hadn't promised my dear husband that I would stop going to school when I turned 50. I still regret that promise!

I've taught in high school (failed miserably), college professor (loved it!), counselor/therapist in agencies and private practice (Omaha, NE,—led some crusades in the '60s and '70s there—very demanding work), and regional-head of a human services agency in Arizona (Phoenix and Tucson—loved it!). Because we lived in Omaha, Tucson, and Phoenix, I have friends in each city, women who will always play a part of my life. They visit us regularly, and we love our secluded lifestyle now (the limelight doesn't have any attraction anymore!). I have also made new friends here in Brushy Creek who grew up with my husband and have known him forever. I retired from official work... and get to do the fun stuff now.

Fun stuff includes...playing piano (since age 4); organ since eighth grade (love classical organ music); and singing, although not solo anymore. I play a beautiful tracker organ at church now (Episcopal church in a nearby town) and love playing church music, too. Gardening...have lots of flowers, shrubs, trees, fruit trees, veg garden and berry bushes)—*keeps me busy and makes the landscape look great as long as I stay ahead of the weeds. Volunteer for American Cancer Society doing a major fundraiser every year and Meals on Wheels when they need me. We live in a forested area of East Texas where most of the roads look like the one the Headless Horseman rode in the Legend of Sleepy Hollow. The townfolk don't know how to get around the hills, so I do delivery of meals to elderly, impoverished folk who live on very little. They delight me and I love to spend time with them.*

I married an enchanting man—Jerry is a retired clergyman; loves taking care of our small homestead; still preaches when invited; is highly known for his pioneering of inner city ministry work in the '60s; has an unending sense of humor; is very bright; and is extremely tolerant and loving with his focused, intent, high-energy wife! He has found great ways to get me to slow down over the years (27 married) and I love him for all his efforts. He had a son from a previous marriage who was 6 when we married; Joel elected to live with us, and I had the great fortune to raise a delightful child (now 35) and he/I claim each other as son/mother. He also has a good relationship with his bio mother; I support that strongly because it is so important to him. Joel is excited to know you have contacted me.

Personal info..I am almost 60; have black & silver hair; 5'5", slim (no chance for flab with the workout I get outside daily!); blue eyes; pets...two loud and raucous daschunds (Keturah & Zechariah-two old testament dogs) and PIA, a feral tabby kitty who adopted us two years ago when he chose this as home (lotsa food!!); also have tons of birds, squirrels, armadillos, rabbits, red foxes, deer and other assorted critters in our forest (we feed everything that needs to eat). The forest is in the piney woods of East Texas, many miles from any civilization. I vote my conscience. People are more important than things; relationships are God's gift to us all and we must treat each gift with extreme care.

I just talked with my dad, 87 yrs old. He lives in Fountain Hills, AZ (my mom died of cancer in 1983). He asked if I had gotten your email, and then wanted me to read it to him.

He said to tell you he loves you.

And I always have loved you.

Sharon

I found it fun sharing her email with my family and close friends. I could not imagine any sourness or negativity about Baby and me. And my feelings proved right. I received congratulatory emails from every member of my family. Their happiness flew into my home and my heart through the telephone and computer lines. All reacted happily about our reunion. Everyone wanted to know the next time I heard from her.

I began to feel that the experience I had in Iowa with my aunts, uncles, and cousins six months earlier had created a path in the universe that had led directly to Baby. With my freedom to live without secrets, Baby somehow knew that the time had arrived to contact me. And she somehow knew that our relationship could begin anew, leaving behind the pain of separation.

Chapter 7

Summer and Fall, 2002
The Long Wait

Tom received the email and sent it on to Baby. I wasn't sleeping much. Not eating much, either. The excitement seemed to fill my head and my stomach so there wasn't room for the normal routine of life. Jerry and I celebrated my birthday that year with a small party at our home with our close friends. They had all heard the story about Baby, and shared our excitement.

One of our friends, a local attorney named Bobby (most East Texas names for men end in a "y"!), listened attentively as I recalled the long-ago experience of Baby's birth, and the recent telephone call from the adoption agency and the email from her.

Tears welled up in Bobby's eyes, and when he could contain them no longer, they spilled over onto his cheeks. He cried, "This is just incredible!"

Our friends' happiness amazed me. No one judged me. They all cried for my good fortune.

I hadn't heard anything more from Tom, but I eagerly checked the computer several times a day for another email. Lots of emails had come in during the week. I reread

Baby's email several times a day, and then reread those from family and friends. I had to keep reviewing everything to make sure I didn't dream it. It takes a long time to change the reality of thirty-six years of separation; the empty place in my heart did not go away immediately. My head had to keep reminding my heart that we walked a new path, toward a reunion. And now the empty place wasn't quite so empty. I dared to hope for its complete disappearance one day.

Tom responded to my email that week. He wanted to assure me that he had sent my email on to Baby.

Sharon,

Received your letter and permission to share everything in your case. Will forward this on to your daughter and get back in touch with you as soon as she responds. She told me she was going on vacation this week but would have a cell phone with her.

Peace,
Tom Lazio

By the end of July, I had heard nothing further. I wanted to believe I'd hear from her again, but in the deeper recesses of my heart, an anxiety began to grow. Perhaps she would never make another contact with me. Perhaps I'd received my one treasured email telling me of her happiness. I wanted to believe differently, but I began to prepare myself for the reality that she might never enter my life again. With growing anxiety and pain, I sent Tom another email.

Date: Tue, 30 Jul 2002 9:8:32 -0500

Tom: ...if you think it appropriate to send this information on to my daughter, you have my permission to do so. (email address change) I have not heard any more from her. I hope that means she is processing this new experience in her life, and not that anything unfortunate has happened to her.

I'm going to AZ next week to visit friends and my father; I keep repeating the "Timing is Everything" mantra.... Thanks for your continuing assistance. -

Sharon Shaw Elrod-

Tom responded.

Thanks for your notes. I'm waiting to hear from your daughter about what she wants to do next. She was very pleased to get your letter.

By way of other news, Alan died last week. Had a chance to visit with his children and share all the good things he did while here. I'll get in touch as soon as I hear something. Tom

Impatience and anxiety took hold. Patience sits at the bottom of my short list of virtues. In fact, I know impatience as a daily companion. I knew I could not create pressure for Baby. She had to write or email or call me because *she* wanted to, not because of my impatience and deep fear about not hearing from her again.

Then, very slowly, the vacillation ceased; impatience

gave way to unending fear and anxiety. By the end of October, I had decided I'd never hear from her again. I believed she communicated what *she* needed to communicate about her life, and that had satisfied her need for contact with me. She simply did not want a relationship with me and I had to determine how to live with that reality. As a happy woman and mother, she did not need her biological mother in her life.

In the hot tub one morning in late October, I told Jerry, "I know I will never hear from her again, and that's okay. I'll live with that. I just have to get used to the idea."

"I'm not so sure about that; I don't know why you haven't heard anything since her first email, but I don't believe that's the last." Jerry was much more optimistic than I.

I wrote Tom one last email, trying desperately to sound matter of fact.

Tom: I'm wondering if you have heard anything from my daughter since early July. You had said she intended to send a letter after her vacation in July; at this point, I have not received anything. Since my email address changed, I just wanted to make sure no communication has fallen through the cracks. Needless to say, I remain eager to get better acquainted, if she chooses to do so. Hope all is well with you.

Sharon

And Tom responded.

Sharon,

Had some computer/virus problems!

Haven't heard from your daughter in a while. Wrote to her and asked if she had any questions or concerns and haven't heard back.

Will get in touch as soon as I hear from her. I know the waiting is hard.

Tom

She did not want or need to communicate with me any more. So I'd learn to accept this reality. I could handle this one more time. I could live with knowing *what* she had chosen to share with me. I had more now than I had before her email. And I had raised some hope for a reunion. She said nothing about reuniting. We'd remain separated and I'd just have to find some way to live with that.

Chapter 8

December 2002
A Christmas Gift

The calendar I keep tells me I had a lot of inconsequential stuff going on that fall. Women's Club meetings, book reviews, a party here and there, weeding and pruning the garden, getting the annuals and perennials ready for winter. The immature plants still required a lot of care prior to the next season. My attempts to keep my sense of desperation under control required incredible energy. I had one email from Baby and she was alive, well, had two children and a loving husband. She's had a good life with the couple entrusted to love her and make her their own. On the outside, I attempted nonchalance with those who asked. But that place in my heart where I kept hopes for a reunion felt hollow and empty. My private fears of a permanent separation prevailed.

In an attempt to buoy my spirits, I dragged out all the holiday decorations from storage. A lot of them. Our barn exceeds 1,600 square feet, and a large part of that area contains boxes of Christmas decorations that go back to the 1960s. I saved everything I ever acquired in adulthood, much to Jerry's dismay. And he saved everything he had ever acquired, adulthood and childhood, much to my dismay. I'd part with his collections, and he with mine, but not our own, so we just keep saving everything. We had boxes upon boxes in storage. And they all came out that year, and we decorated the house from top to bottom. I needed old stuff and lifetime memories around me to try to fill the empty place in my heart.

The glitz and glamour looked spectacular. We had toy trains on tables, birds' nests in gilded baskets, ornaments from Europe hung on strings of gold and silver wire. All over the house we placed holiday pieces we had collected from the cities and homes in which we had lived. Omaha and Tucson and Phoenix, and now East Texas. We had old stuff and new, dog-eared and shiny, and a towering 16-foot tree that we found locally a couple of years previously. We placed it just inside the front door and covered it with all the tree decorations we had. And we put ten strings of tiny Christmas tree lights on it. The overdone décor served as testimony to my sense of loss once again.

We entered the last week before Christmas. Our son, Joel, joined us and we had a wonderful time with him. He and I connected very early in his life, and he has always considered me "Mom." When the telephone rings late at night or early morning, or any unusual time, I know it's Joel, and he needs to talk. I always shut everything down and just listen and respond when he calls. I know from my experience with Joel, and with Baby, that biology does not make a parent.

Joel was leaving to spend the rest of his holiday with his mother and we sent him off too soon for our preferences. Jerry and I had spent a fun day together. With unusually warm weather, we had spent some time outside, a gift from unusual winters that sometimes descend upon East Texas. Not unlike that day five months earlier, we walked in from having spent some time outside in the garden, and the telephone rang as I prepared lunch in the kitchen. It was Tom.

He called on December 12, 2002. "Hi, Sharon, this is Tom Lazio, and I have a Christmas present for you."

This time my heart didn't pound. It stopped. My ears weren't working well; the disbelief flooded my senses; I had consciously to tell my lungs to take in a breath.

I heard bits and pieces of what Tom said, "...your daughter...might be traveling...holidays...approaching ...heads up...another email..." Once I started breathing again, the tears flowed. I could hear Tom's smile on the other end of the line.

"Go ahead, Sharon. You've waited so long for this. Your tears make sense right now." So, of course, with such tender permission, I just sat down and wept for unutterable joy.

And how does one prepare for another email, knowing that it might be the last one...again? But I entertained that thought only for a moment. All my lifetime hopes and dreams once again rushed to the surface. Another email from Baby! How absolutely and totally incredible!

I have since discovered that Baby has absolutely no sense of time. She never did. Anyone who takes 36 hours to come into this world cannot concern herself about time. She has many more important things to think about. The email did not arrive until several days later.

However, in her defense, it probably was not her fault.

I had changed my email address a month or so before Christmas, and Tom had not given her my new one. So it wasn't until December 17 that her email arrived. Strangely, I did not get anxious about the delay this time. I only attributed it to the email address mix-up. No anxiety, no fear; impatience had returned with a vengeance!

I checked the monitor every few minutes during that time. No sleep. No food. Incredibly impatient. The whole routine all over again. Jerry tolerated my obsessing so well. He even asked several times if it had arrived yet. He felt almost as eager as I to hear from her. Jerry had told me for 36 years that she'd contact me one day. He never had any doubts. But I couldn't let myself hope incessantly for those 36 years. The small empty place in my heart wouldn't let me.

I turned the volume on the computer speakers as high as possible. Every time it said, "You've got mail" I ran to the library. And for two days my sisters, my aunts, and my close friends wrote to see if Baby's email had arrived yet. My response each time: "Still waiting." And then, one last time, late Tuesday night, when the computer said, "You've got mail," I was sound asleep.

Early Wednesday morning, I again stumbled to the library to check the monitor. I saw it. "hello (not junk mail!)." I didn't recognize the email address, but I knew it was Baby's. No, my child; it certainly is not junk mail. It is incredibly precious and treasured—probably the most important piece of mail ever written in history. Definitely not junk mail.

I screamed for Jerry. The deeply shared love we have for each other propelled him to the same heights of emotion that I experienced. Just as Joel and I connected because Jerry chose to share his life with me, Baby would be Jerry's child. We laughed and cried and hugged, celebrating our first contact with our daughter, our real daughter, no longer a phantom hope.

And then she had a name. We sat and looked at the monitor for a few seconds before I clicked on the email. I'd received *the first* message I had ever received directly from her. I needed to relish this life-changing moment.

Jerry whispered, "Click on the message when you're ready." "Ready?" I thought, "I have been ready for 36 years."

Fear and anxiety vanished the instant I saw her message on the screen.

12/17/02 11:32:48 PM
Subject: hello (not junk mail!)

Dear Sharon -

I wrote the letter below on Sunday—had a bit of trouble getting your correct email address...!

Once again, I find myself at a loss for words (a situation that rarely happens to me!) when trying to start a letter to you. I spoke with Tom Lazio at American Home Finding yesterday, and he gave me your home address and email. I thought it might be a little easier to send you an email to begin with...

I guess I just wanted to say hi, and let you know I'm thinking of you and your family. Your letter really touched me, and I treasure it—an amazing coincidence (although I don't believe anything is really a coincidence) is that you had said your father lives in Fountain Hills. I live in Scottsdale, just over the ridge from Fountain Hills; your father must live less than 5 minutes from me!

Please write back when you have time - I feel how much energy and emotion it takes to correspond like this, and if you feel you can't do it until after the holiday season, I understand! I truly look forward to hearing from you. As Tom said, it's important to not rush, but I trust that things will work out exactly as they should!

With love,

Kate

After the holiday season, Ha! It took me all of five seconds to start my response.

Dear Kate:

I cannot tell you how hearing from you again thrilled me! I told Tom of my email change last August (and several times since!) but feared he hadn't made the change on his computer. So I am relieved to know you now have the correction.

Our beliefs about life and living sound very similar. I don't believe God uses a chess board to control and direct our lives; but I do believe it's up to us to respond to life events and experiences with honor, wisdom and love. I offer that to you as the foundation for whatever relationship we mutually choose to develop. And the choices will always be in your hands. I've wanted you and your family in my life for a long time; but I know you have to feel comfortable and ready for however we proceed.

48

This is the best holiday I could have hoped for! Tom said you may be traveling over the holidays, and if you are in Texas, and if you feel ready, I'd love to see you—and your family, if you want to include them. You are invited to our home (maps & directions are essential!) or I would meet you anywhere within 100,000 miles! We are within two hours of Dallas, three hours of Houston and about four of Austin.

I just talked with my father and told him you probably lived within 5 minutes of him... and he almost cried. He said he wanted to see you, too—and then stumbled all over his words saying, "I'll go to her home; she can come here (to FH); I'll meet her somewhere in Scottsdale... I really want to see her!!" He was really funny and we both ended up laughing. If/when you are ready to look at some pictures, you can see him, our home, and me, two of my sisters, my son (Joel) on my personal web site—

I am attaching a holiday greeting from Jerry and me. Again, if you are not ready for all that (including a picture of us), that's okay and I understand. I'm trying not to write an epistle and overwhelm you! (I can do that before I even know what I've done!) I am just very excited that we are in touch with each other. Proceeding slowly is something I've never done very well, but I agree with Tom that we need to make sure that we don't rush this experience. I really look forward to hearing from you again.

My love to you and yours,
Sharon

Chapter 9

Christmas, 2002
Emails and Pictures

Words simply cannot describe my feelings. A lifetime of hoping, wanting to get a glimpse of what she looked like, wishing to talk with her, weeping over not knowing her, struggling with the desire to share feelings and life and dreams and memories, fruitless empty desire. All that had ended, suddenly and miraculously. No longer wondering. Wishes turning into reality. Replaced by unbounded joy. All of life in front of me rather than behind me. Incredible joy overwhelmed me.

I sat at the computer over an hour, rereading her message. She existed. She had a name. Kate. No longer Rachael Ann. No longer nameless. No longer a phantom hope. But Kate. And always Baby.

The keyboard almost caved in over the next several hours. I emailed everyone! Sisters, close friends like sisters, family, aunts, uncles, cousins, and friends who told me they wanted to hear from me when I got her next message. Their responses vibrated with the disbelief I felt. They all knew how long I had waited and how deeply I desired to hear. And I discovered all over again how joy deepens when we share it with those we love.

That day carries some blurry places for me. I think I couldn't process it all and my psyche just shut down at times. My memory, however, sees me returning to the computer too many times to count, to reread her message. A small part of me did not yet believe. And then another part took over and wanted to hear more about her and read more of her messages—messages that she wrote to *me*. Absolutely incredible!

That night I walked around the house looking at the beauty the holiday décor had brought into our home, basking in my newfound *joie de vivre* that had permeated my consciousness, then the computer said, "You've got mail." I raced to the library, knowing it was another message from Kate.

I was thrilled to hear from you so quickly - not having much patience myself, I've spent a lot of time today looking at your letter, website... Have to say, I've enjoyed it immensely! ...I'm attaching the photo of my kids that I sent out with our Christmas cards... since I get the feeling we'll be writing a lot, I'll sign off now and attach those photos...

With love,
Kate

She already knew what I needed and wanted to hear. How? *Writing a lot...thrilled to hear from you...enjoyed it immensely... with love.* And now pictures! I screamed for Jerry as I clicked on the attached file.

The computer moved slower than a turtle. I wanted to

see pictures of *my* grandchildren -- for the first time in my life. I'm sure the feeling matched what any grandparent experiences. Only my grandbabes, at seven and nine years old, were not babies. My new happiness refused to let me dwell on what I had missed out on; I wanted only to look at what I had gained in the click of a mouse on an attached file.

And then they appeared. Absolutely the most beautiful children ever warmed by the sun in all of civilization. A handsome, smiling boy with a smile I recognized and a glint in his eye that could only reflect a dynamic personality. And a beautiful angelic little girl whose eyes and nose appeared so familiar and whose smile reflected happiness and goodness unmeasured.

My grandbabes. I whispered through happy tears, "Oh, Jerry; they are so beautiful! So perfect!" As I rose to get the photo paper, Jerry sat down, and for the first time looked at our grandchildren. He immediately noticed genetic similarities and rapidly pointed them out to me. Eyes, nose, smile. The black-and-white picture left us unsure of their hair color. My sisters and I all had dark brown or black hair and I knew that was recessive in genetics. I would be surprised if their hair was as dark as mine. I printed the picture as large as the paper allowed.

The next photo showed Brad and Tina and Kate. I saw Baby for the first time since her birth. In retrospect, I know it took days for reality to really sink in. However, I remember sitting at the computer and thinking, this is Baby. This is a picture of my daughter. I no longer have to conjure images of what she looks like. I see what she looks like, here and now.

The impact of all that I experienced was just too much to take in at one time. My mind thought something very logical, such as, "This is a picture of Kate." But my feelings screamed. *A picture of my daughter! Of Baby! Absolutely unbelievable!* I'd leap from joy and laughter to tears and sobbing in seconds. I just could not assimilate it all. Then I realized that the emotions lagged far behind reality, moving much slower than the day-to-day experience Kate and I would share. My feelings moved behind what my mind now knew as real and tangible and here and now.

Without question, she was my daughter. Genetics do not lie. I have never taken credit for my physical appearance, nor is it important to me; after all, it's all genetic. But suddenly, my appearance took center stage. Baby actually looked like me. In fact, I had a picture in a photo album, one among thirty or more on a shelf in the library. I wore similar colors. Our resemblance is phenomenal. I tucked away a mental reminder to dig out that picture and send her a copy. I could now begin thinking those kinds of thoughts. Oh, by the way, I'll have to send that to Kate. *Incredible!*

Kate looked like me. Oddly, I remember thinking; I wonder if others will notice. What strange thoughts surface in the midst of emotional exhilaration! I had copied all the pictures she attached, and then spent the next hour looking from one to the next to the next. I looked at pictures of my daughter. Of my grandbabes. Of my family. Of our family.

Christmas neared. But I took time the next day to drive an hour to find frames for the pictures. I had to have them on display in our home. Jerry went with me and we had other errands to run. I felt impatient again! Still! I wanted to get home to get the pictures in their frames, and put them where they belonged. One in the library. One in the media room. And one by my bedside.

And finally I got them in place. Our home welcomed the pictures and wrapped its loving arms around our newfound family. I'd always saved a place for them, and now each place was filled with the unprecedented joy of their presence.

I sat down at the computer again to compose the next communication to Kate. She and her family were not going to travel over the holidays; they were staying in Scottsdale. I needed to tell her about her bio-family in Scottsdale. She wanted to know about her bio-grandfather living only five minutes away. I began telling her about her bio-aunt living only five minutes away, and her bio-cousin living only five minutes away…

… I want to tell you about …my niece, who lives in Fountain Hills… an attorney… her husband…a stay-at-home dad… three children. You and Ann share your birthdays, and you were born about 2 hours apart; she weighed two ounces more than you did, and you looked like you could have been twins… she is very eager to meet you. She probably lives within 5 minutes of you. Her telephone number… And you are right, dear love, there aren't any coincidences in my life either.

Gotta go find the Kleenex. More later...
Love you,
Sharon

I hoped I wasn't overwhelming Kate. I never mastered the tricky balance between sharing information and coming on too strong. In fact, coming on too strong and too fast with too much information aptly described my style!

But it didn't faze Kate. She loved hearing about her bio-family. She considered them *my* family, and I understood that. If she never considered them *her* family, I'd be all right with that. She had to control how we developed our relationship. I'd do *nothing* in the world to interfere with her sense of safety in our relationship. She was far too important to me to ever do that.

I love hearing about your family, and am excited to meet all of them I have to say, the information... floored me!!! I can't wait to meet her; perhaps I already have?! Please let them all know that I'll get in touch after the holidays.

I'm planning on taking some digital photos during the next week (especially Christmas day!) & I'll send any decent ones on to you. Please send me any more that you have, or that you take during the holidays!

With Love,
Kate

Sharing pictures made up our first attempt to do normal things together. It comforted me. It felt right and good. I looked forward to a wonderful holiday season and evenings with friends. We hosted our annual open house on January 1, complete with Southern New Year's Day traditions of black-eyed peas, greens and cornbread. Cousin Lyn and her husband and my Aunt Dori from San Diego planned to come and spend a wonderful week with us.

And then Christmas Eve, I felt melancholy. Not sad. Not depressed. Just melancholy. So I did the only logical thing I could do. I emailed Kate.

Merry Christmas to you and your loved ones...

I know you are enjoying a wonderful family time, as are we. Please know that your family will always be honored and respected by me and all the Shaws and Elrods. We will never interfere; but we hope to enhance...I finally found a picture today that I have been looking for... and I am attaching it... taken by my sister in her home in November, 1996... a most blessed and happy holiday to you all, with much love to each of you... and especially your wonderful parents...

Sharon

I offered her reassurance that I needed myself. I needed her to know she'd be perfectly safe with me and with my family, that we had no desire to interfere in any way with her family. I had to make sure she knew that.

Jerry also wanted to communicate with Kate. Christmas is a time for sharing special joy, and Jerry began to know the feelings of a dad for his daughter. And he found that he needed to share the joy of his new fatherhood experience...

Please forgive me for invading your very busy Christmas, but I felt the strong need to share some of my own feelings about all of what has occurred in the past week.

With your permission, I want to join Sharon in expressing our mutual exhilaration at your entry into our lives. Sharon and I have been married 27 years, having known each other for years before that. We first met when she worked with a non-profit agency on whose board I sat. She and my first wife enjoyed a close friendship. Sharon literally has known my (our) son, Joel, all his life.

Good fortune prevailed when in 1974 Joel chose to live with me. My marriage had ended in 1970. Sharon and I married on August 31, 1975, with Joel participating in the service. It remains a mystical union. We feel thrice blessed, and now your coming into our lives has quadrupled our life's experience in ways we might never have known.

And now to you. Your entry into our lives is the fruition of a dream onto which Sharon has held tenaciously for all these years. I knew this experience would come to pass. That it has speaks volumes. It says a great deal about the human being you have become. I admire, respect and hold the deepest affection for you. It tells me that you are, like your biological mother, a person who is immensely self assured, enormously sensitive and affectionate, unequivocally accepting and remarkably adventurous. For my part, I am so utterly grateful to be a part of this part of the adventure.

Adding you and your family to the circle of those whose lives are most precious to us simply enlarges our own lives. Thank you for this wonderful, marvelous, generous gift.

My love and cherished admiration,
Jerry

Christmas absolutely thrilled me! I felt better than a ten-year-old opening my stocking and gifts and knowing Santa Claus was a spirit and not a human person, and loving the day anyway! I walked around the house looking at pictures of Kate and the children and loved the sense of well being I felt when I looked at them. Life just could not get any better than this!

The day after Christmas, another email came.

It was so much fun to read even more about your family!!! I can't wait to meet Ann and Brett & their kiddies, as well as your sister & father. I must say, the fates make all this quite easy and convenient, with half your family within a few miles of me... :)

I'll watch for emails and photos... feel free to share mine with anyone who cares to know it... Just tell them to put something in the subject line that'll keep me from hitting 'delete' before reading it! Also, I guess I need to say that I also will be 100% respectful of the fact that I am essentially a stranger to your family, and will not interfere with anyone or any relationships that don't/can't include me. I truly have an amazing life, for which I try to be grateful every moment, and I feel like I must have some fabulous karma going to deserve so many blessings right now!

Kate and I both experienced the same kinds of feelings. We felt amazingly blessed at our spectacular reunion. She felt safer. She believed my reassurances and learned I would never do anything to harm her or her family. She and her husband took the children skiing and she took her computer along. So our emails kept going back and forth through Christmas break. I kept sharing our emails, news, pictures, and information with friends and family. And we began making plans for our first meeting.

Chapter 10

January 2003
Getting Ready to Meet

In January, after getting all the holiday decorations boxed and stored, life supposedly slows down again to a normal pace and a sense of relaxation sets in. We start thinking about taking that legendary long winter's nap. HA! I started to realize that I'd have to redefine normal. My future life looked very different from the previous one. Nothing would ever be normal again. Well…not so. Life *would* be normal again, with the new normal forever and always very unlike the first six decades of my life.

I still awoke every morning with a sense of exhilaration. Baby and her family existed in my life, and I began to allow myself to hope and to believe in a future with them. I had talked with my closest friends at the end of our New Year open house. They'd wept and laughed and shared the joy over my news that my daughter wanted to have me in her life again. My story brought incredible tears of joy to the eyes of everyone I call friend in this world.

My normal day now included looking at Kate's picture, at the pictures of my grandchildren, my son-in-law, normal stuff like pictures of their day in DisneyWorld and on the ski slopes in Arizona. Normal stuff like reading Kate's emails, and sending emails to her. Just like any mother communicated with her daughter. Normal mother and daughter stuff.

Jerry and I faced a major decision. We usually traveled to Arizona after the first of the year to see my father and other family members, and close friends from our 12 years of living there. I wanted to make that trip again in January or February, but I also had a desperate need to see Kate and her family as soon as possible. And I had to tread very carefully so as not to scare her by pushing for a reunion too fast. I agonized over the decision, but I had to go to Arizona. And I had to tell her we were coming. And I had to tell her I'd accept her decision if she didn't want to see me yet. I could wait for her plans, if she needed more time. However, in that secret place in my heart, I counted on genetics! Her reply was textbook Shaw-Baby stuff!

It seems like there is so much information to exchange that it's almost overwhelming! Please ask me anything you'd like to know; I don't have any qualms about answering anything you want to ask. I was trying to decide how I feel about your trip here this month, and realized that it'd be impossible for me to know you were a couple miles away and not plan to see you. So, let me know when & where you'll be! Actually, I think I may throw a party and invite all of your family. Anyone else planning on coming here then?!

Most of my family shares behavior traits that I call Shaw Behavior. We meet challenges eagerly, with confidence. We're able to show some wisdom, seldom fearful, and we always desire to know the unknown. Kate responded in a fashion typical of her genetic relatives: *When in doubt, throw a party!!*

As I began to pack my suitcase I decided I needed a whole new wardrobe. With little time to shop, Jerry and I made a speedy trip to Tyler, looking for that perfect item to wear when I saw Kate for the first time in our adult lives. The pantsuit jumped out at me in the first department store. My size. Bought it and drove back home. Forget a new wardrobe. Life is even too exciting to shop!

Baby also prepared. She shared personal information; I knew she felt confident that I would not hurt her or her family…

Random bits of info Brad's birthday is… Tina's is… Full names - … Tina got her nickname… I'm not sure how much info you've gotten over the years from AHFA and/or Tom Lazio so if I repeat anything you already know, sorry! Dogs are… Two cats… Also have horses (NOT in the back yard), fish, and a gerbil… Guess I don't need to explain why my friends call me Mother Nature!

Love,
Kate

I told Kate of a plan in place for the past couple of years for a Shaw Family Reunion at our home, Concord Lodge, sometime in 2003. The reunion turned into a tradition in the past decade; the cousins in Kate's generation had insisted on a get-together every two or three years, and so far my sisters and I had managed to meet their demands.

I visited my sister, Pat, and her daughter, Jill, when I went through Iowa in January 2002. They have a snazzy coffee shop in Johnston, Iowa, a suburb of Des Moines. Jill put pressure on me about the reunion, reminding me that Jerry and I had agreed to host it at Concord Lodge. As we talked, I reminded her I'd also have a birthday in July of 2003, and asked if she'd permit us to celebrate my birthday with the reunion. Her startling, deep-set brown eyes flashed with excitement, "Of course! We need to help you celebrate going over the hill at 60!" So the Shaw-Bang turned into a celebration combined with my birthday.

The 2003 reunion fell in place, and every biological descendant of my mother and father planned to come. Now Kate and her husband and my grandbabes were included.

I definitely think I'm going to try and plan to come out to Texas for your birthday bash. Let me know the details when you have them.

Yes, indeed; Kate was a Shaw Baby! Issue her an invitation that includes a challenge, and she grabs it like a walleye pike on a minnow.

So now we had our meet-up planned for late January, and my daughter and her family made plans to come for her bio-family reunion in July. Somehow during all this exchange of emails, I found language that made sense to me…didn't have to make sense to the rest of the world, just had to sound respectful and appropriate. The Shaws are her bio-family, I am her bio-mother, Jerry is her b/s (bio-step)-dad (hee!), and everyone else has to figure out their labels!!

Seemed to work for us.

A new wrinkle developed before Jerry and I finally made it to Arizona. Kate and Ann had made email contact, and planned to get together. Ann didn't want to tread on my territory and meet Kate before I did, but she chomped at the bit to get acquainted. I happily gave my permission for them to get together whenever they could, and they grabbed the opportunity.

They met at a local café, and recognized each other immediately. Had an evening full of comparing information about their lives, questions asked and answered, and the beginnings of a familial bond. They talked about their kids, about the Shaw family, and talked about their lives as accomplished women.

Ann called me late that evening after she got home, and told me about the amazing time she and Kate experienced. She told me she could see me in Kate. She told me they shared a lot of common life experiences -- getting a shag haircut in third grade, getting glasses in fourth grade, getting ribbed throughout school because of their brains. They began to bridge the time-gap between their birth dates and now.

Kate sent a more explicit and detailed email.

Hi Sharon!

Well, Ann said she was heading home to call you after our dinner last night. I was a little leery of what she might say, but decided that whatever it is, it's the truth so you might as well know it now! Just hope she didn't say I was a total flake...

I had a terrific time meeting her. Very fun, very easy just more confirmation that this is exactly as it is supposed to be. We're taking off in a few hours to go to San Diego for the long weekend. I'm planning on taking my laptop so I can check for more emails!

Please pass the word around; the party will start at 4 on Saturday the 1st at my place. Very casual, snacks & drinks & maybe we'll break out the barbecue for dinner or order pizza if we're feeling exceptionally lazy. Pizza may be preferred, as I don't put meat on my barbecue and don't think EVERYONE likes tofu dogs and soy patties as much as we do!!! Our address is... I can send directions to anyone who needs them. Our home phone is... and my cell is... I usually send out paper invitations for parties so I hope this is sufficient! Anyone who needs more info is welcome to call or email.

Love,
Kate

Jerry and I made our final plans for the trip to Phoenix. We planned to fly. Sister Marlene said she'd meet us at the airport, and we'd journey through the beautiful Indian Reservation land to Fountain Hills to stay with Dad and his wife. Sleep escaped me. Kept thinking through wardrobe, approach, low-key stuff, don't push, show love, do everything perfectly. Kept trying to find all the right keys and all the right answers so that I wouldn't muck up our meet-up.

Kate, her husband, and kids had gone skiing. They

weren't at home. I made an impulsive decision and called their home number. Decided if I were meeting someone for the first time that I was connected to biologically, I might appreciate a little heads-up. So I called their home. And then sent an email…

Hi!

Just got back from our evening walk 'n talk… which we do every evening around some of our 67 acres (Jerry and I walk, and talk about our life experience each day…and much of it for the past month has been about you and me.) And decided I wanted to tell you that I took advantage of your being away from home this weekend, and called your home number and left a msg… that says we're excited about coming to AZ and can't wait to see you and we love you all… Just wanted to try to finish chipping away at the little bit of frozen water that is left before we finally see each other… the experience has been very good for me so far, and your emails suggest it has been for you, too… just want our first voice contact and face contact to be a continuation of what we have begun this past month. The journey has been a long one, and as you have told me several times, everything is happening as it should be happening. I am beyond thrilled… and into grace… you and your family are a gift of grace… and we are so eager to hug you all…

Sharon

Chapter 11

January 28, 2003
In Person, at Last!

January 28, 2003, a Tuesday, dawned clear, pristine, and cold in Texas. Jerry and I boarded the plane without incident. My fears of an international incident that prohibited travel of any kind proved unfounded—just overactive worry. We arrived at Phoenix Sky Harbor. Marlene met us and we had our usual fun reunion and catch-up on the way northeast to Fountain Hills.

She helped us into Dad's home, suitcases and cherished beige-silk suit in hand. Kate instructed me to call her on her cell to schedule our reunion. I wasn't sure what the reunion looked like in her mind, so I placed the call—fingers trembling. She answered, "Hi...it's Kate." I heard her voice for the first time in my life (well, her voice with words for the first time.) Time stopped.

When I finally realized I had to say something, I said, "Hi...it's Sharon." She greeted me warmly and we agreed to meet that evening at 6:15. My first telephone conversation with Kate! I had to get used to all the "firsts"!

The next several hours I count among the most frenetic in my life. For some inexplicable reason, my appearance became important to me on January 28, 2003. I had to *look* perfect. So Jeannine and Marlene came into the bedroom with me and, much as we had as little girls, we primped and preened and did hair, and re-did makeup and did more preening and primping until I feel embarrassed to say more. I finally emerged from the bedroom only to discover I wasn't wearing shoes. The shoes didn't go with the beige silk pantsuit. We tried on several different pairs of shoes, and nothing worked, so I went with the least offensive ones I had. I only hoped Kate wouldn't notice my imperfect shoes.

Time moved very slowly, but the clock finally read 6 straight up. I picked up the keys to Daddy's car, hugged Jerry, my sisters, Daddy and Delilah, and went out to the car. Eternally optimistic, I had decided Kate and I would have a good reunion. I merely had to stop feeling like a five-year-old about to get on the biggest roller coaster on the planet.

I drove to the restaurant, only eight minutes away from Daddy's house. I did my deep breathing exercises. I kept my heart beating as slowly as possible, my respiration rate low. This was going to be one of the most important moments in my life, and I was going to handle it honorably. Breathe slowly.

I pulled into the parking lot and tried not to look at a young woman walking toward the door. Got out of the car and walked eagerly toward the restaurant. I knew I was about to see Baby for the first time since her birth. I had to hold on to the moment

The restaurant had a typical small foyer before entry into the restaurant proper, so I walked through the first set of doors, then opened the second set of doors, and walked through. Lots of people sat at tables in the dimly lit restaurant. I looked around trying to see someone who looked like the pictures I had on my computer and in frames around my home. As I peered through the crowd in the restaurant, I felt a hand on my left shoulder.

Jerry chides me for never seeing the obvious. I always look in places where I will not find what I seek.

I turned to my left and saw my daughter. Beautiful. Smiling. Tears welling up in her eyes. Blue eyes. My eyes. Her eyes. Identical eyes. Perfect.

We fell into each other's arms. I have no clue how long the hug lasted. Comprehension was not high on my priority list at that moment. The inexplicable experience of holding Kate in my arms again isn't comprehendible. Such joy has no words.

I clutched a few times with sobs, and then had to look at her again. We held each other and looked into an almost mirror image of our own faces. Tears began to overflow on my face, and she lovingly protested, "Don't do that to me! I don't cry and you're making me cry!"

I thought, what do we do now? I don't want to let her go. We giggled over our tears, ordered a glass of wine, and sat down.

Getting reacquainted after 36 years felt just about perfect. I learned about her children, Brad and Christina, her husband, and her life. Realization slowly dawning...*my* grandchildren, *my* son-in-law, *my* daughter's life. She loves animals and I learned about her experiences with them. Her very dear friend's automobile accident brought Kate a sense of mild urgency about contacting me; she realized she did not want to wait too long and regret never knowing me.

Our first conversation, in retrospect, heralded our similarities. She shared her belief that our lives evolve along a path that, although we make our own choices, nonetheless includes an Unseen Companion who shares the journey with us and who ensures that life unfolds exactly as it should. I have always believed that God doesn't move us humans around on a chessboard and play games with our lives, but that the spirit of God stays with us, with all our choices and decisions, and *is* the Spirit of Love. We share similar belief systems that include facets of eastern religions. Our common love for the work and writings of Deepak Chopra made for another startling revelation.

I asked questions; Kate asked questions; we both answered them so easily and so honestly. She assured me she *never* felt anything negative toward me. Her parents had done an exceptional and wonderful job convincing her she was placed for adoption because her mother loved her, not because her mother dumped and did not care for her. She does not feel that she missed out on anything. She considers me and her bio-family a *bonus*. Life has been great for her, and now she just got some whipped cream topping with chocolate crumbles!

We had talked over two hours, and Kate suddenly announced, "I'm hungry!"

We had been drinking wine and eating nothing. In fact we had forgotten about eating. But by then our excitement over our reunion dulled just enough to allow the hunger pangs to push through. Kate had told me she is vegetarian. Another similarity! Although not totally vegetarian (I eat fish and poultry), I try not to eat any other animal protein; I have fibro-cystic breast disease and it causes lumps; Kate inherited FCBD from me, and I was so grateful she chose a vegetarian diet.

After a plate of lettuce wraps and pasta, I invited Kate to come back to Daddy's and meet the family that had gathered there.

Her response? "Sure! Let's go!" Definitely a Shaw baby!

The climax of the night of our first meet-up occurred when we drove onto the driveway at Daddy's and saw Jerry standing there waiting for us. I had called ahead to let them know WE were coming back together.

Jeannine answered. "You're on your way home? You're both on your way? You both are coming here? Now?" She screamed into the phone.

By that time I felt relatively calm, and simply answered, "Yes. Five minutes." And ended the call.

Jerry stood on the driveway with tears streaming down his face, big smile and arms wide open. He always knew this day would come, even when I dared not hope. He always knew he'd one day welcome Baby into our family. The day arrived. And he had to be there, outside, to greet Kate before she met the rest of her bio-family.

We walked into the house through the open garage door and into the kitchen. They all stood there waiting for us. I hadn't rehearsed this. I stumbled through what to say. How do you introduce your daughter to her bio-family?

"Well…here we are!" I could manage no more. Kate and Jerry stood behind me, arms around each other. My family laughed gently at my feeble attempt to start the introductions.

"This is Kate!" came my next equally feeble statement. Big smiles and teary eyes all around. She and Ann hugged again, having already met. Then sisters and spouses. And then Daddy.

"Kate, this is your grandpa." For the first time in their lives, they greeted and hugged and loved. More tears. And Daddy's wife showed equal thrill at welcoming Kate into the Shaw family.

We got another glass of wine and went into the great room and talked for another two hours. I thought our family peppered Kate with questions, but she later recounted the evening and said she hadn't felt under scrutiny at all. She enjoyed getting acquainted with all there, and she felt welcomed and loved by each one.

As she later said, we both experienced the evolving of our lives, exactly as they were supposed to evolve.

Chapter 12

January 29, 2003
Grandchildren

Stories like these frequently include the cliché, "That time blurs in my mind." Well, nothing blurs for me about that time in Arizona with Kate and family. I remember almost every detail. The time held far too much importance for me to ever forget.

During our first meeting, I had suggested Kate's family and Jerry and I meet for dinner the next evening. Jerry and I wanted eagerly to meet the rest of her family. She suggested we come over to their home, meet the children and her husband and then go out to dinner.

An early concern of mine centered around how the children would learn about our reunion, and what they'd call me. They knew of Kate's adoption and knew the children's version of what that meant. I needed to stay on course and focus on not interfering in their lives. Throughout my entire journey, I made that my primary concern. I wanted to avoid creating distress for Kate and her family.

Kate decided to tell them after they returned home from school that afternoon. She reminded them about the adoption story, and then told them she had found her bio-mother, and that we'd all eat dinner together that evening.

Kate reports that Brad said, "Cool!"

And Tina said, "Omigod! I have to take a shower and wash my hair! What will I wear? How much time do I have?" All this as she ran to her bathroom and the shower! Typical Shaw baby behavior, even for an eight-year-old!

Jerry and I spent that day in warm afterglow. We talked with each other and family about our evening with Kate as we all tried to adjust to the new set of emotions in our lives. Incredulity slowly gave way to excited acceptance of welcoming Kate into the family.

Daddy shook his head several times in wonderment. We all wiped tears from our eyes as we talked. Everyone hugged me a lot and told me how happy they felt for me and for themselves. And we all anticipated the upcoming evening, Jerry and I meeting our grandbabes for the first time. I had the sense that a lot of the happiness my family expressed came from knowing that I no longer had to live with all the losses that resulted from having placed Kate for adoption. They knew, as did I, that the losses had disappeared with Kate's courageous decision.

Kate had given us directions to her home. She timed the drive at 12 minutes from Daddy's. She timed it right.

A little before 5:30 we pulled up in front of their home. Jerry stepped out of the car laughing. I wondered at the time why.

I saw two little guys running from the front of the house to previously identified hiding spots behind shrubs and a pillar on the front of the house. They ran fast enough that I couldn't get a good look at them.

We walked toward the house. Kate and her husband came out the front door. Big smiles and hugs and introductions. We all felt happiness at meeting.

"Brad, Tina, come on out now," Kate called.

And then those two most beautiful children in the world slowly came out of their hiding spots and slowly walked to us. They were the children in the picture that sat in my home, with my eyes and my smile. *My grandchildren.*

"Brad and Tina, this is Sharon and Jerry," Kate made the introduction look so easy and comfortable. Big smiles all around.

Tina stood in front; I held out my arms to her and she immediately threw hers around my neck. I only remember holding her and wishing for time to stop. Whether the child's an infant, or eight years old, the first experience holding a grandchild is spiritual. I knew that she'd participate in my immortality. And such a beautiful child to do so!

When our embrace slowly dissolved, I turned to Brad. I sensed that in his transition from childhood into pre-puberty, he wasn't sure about greeting style. I shared the uncertainty.

So I asked, "Brad, do you hug or shake hands?"

Only a short pause, and then, "Both!" I thought, "Typical Shaw baby," as we shook hands before he jumped into my arms. I then discovered why Jerry laughed as we exited the car. He wanted to communicate safety and approachability. The children heard him loud and clear!

We enjoyed a wonderful dinner. Our first dinner with our daughter and her family! We went to a kid-friendly

75

place where Brad & Tina could play with pasta dough, color on the food mats, and run around the play area with the rest of the kids.

Jerry and I love calamari, so we ordered an hors d'oeuvres dish for us. Kate chose cheese sticks. When the waiter served it, we carefully kept the vegetarian hors d'oeuvres separated from the calamari. Brad didn't want them touching!

For the entree, Jerry and I chose linguine with clam sauce; the kids wanted pizza. Kate & her husband ordered fettuccine alfredo. We talked with our daughter and her husband and asked more questions and related more life experiences as we waited for dinner. Love just kept growing with the restated and accepted promise never to injure again.

Chapter 13

January 31, 2003
More Family Meet-ups

Even though Kate's party was scheduled for Saturday, February 1, we decided we wanted another family time together and gathered Friday evening for a pizza dinner, again, kid-friendly!

In addition to Brad and Tina, Ann's children joined with us. By this time, family had arrived from California and Iowa. When I thought about the part of my family that lived in Arizona, I wondered at Kate's proximity to them. Coincidence?

Kate and family came to Daddy's home that evening so the children could meet their great-grandpa before the large group gathered. They also wanted to see Great-Grandpa's house. Brad and Tina began to understand the story of their biological family. We visited briefly and then left for the pizza parlor. The rest of the family waited for us there. Introductions challenged us with five children and 15 adults, all very hungry!

My cousins and aunt from California had arrived, and our son, Joel, made the trip from San Francisco. They all took Kate up on her invitation to c'mon and enjoy a party! Some cousins are more like sisters in our family, so it felt normal for them to participate.

Aunt Dori, one of my mother's younger sisters, flew in from San Diego to join the extended family reunion. When she first heard the story about Baby and adoption, her response meant more to me than she could ever know. She emailed six months previously,

Dear Sharon,

I am happy to hear your news. I'm sure this has been a heavy burden to carry for this many years. Not only for you but for your dad and your mom. I'm sure she can see the heartache this has caused you and regrets a decision they made. She loved you, and sometimes in trying to do what they thought best, they made a mistake of a lifetime. I pray that you get the chance to accept and forgive the terrible wrong you endured. God loves you and accepts you. We all do, and wish the best for you.

All my love, Aunt Doris

Her message felt like a message from my mother. She told me on her deathbed that she hoped I'd reunite with Baby someday. How I wished she had lived to see it happen. But Aunt Dori sat in for Mom. What a thrill to experience my mother's presence in my aunt! And Aunt Dori reciprocated that weekend, telling me I was like a daughter to her. How incredible to have a mother again! I felt my mother's strong love for me coming through my aunt.

Big smiles. Lots of hugs. Not a lot of time for serious talking, but just good family time together. Nothing unusual or out of the ordinary for a family getting together, for a meal and a pleasant evening together. We talked some about the party the next day. Kate politely refused offers of help. She had it all under control.

Chapter 14

February 1, 2003
Disaster and Delight, strange partners

No one in the world could have predicted, nor expected, the disaster that occurred on that Saturday morning. I awakened late, probably because my adrenaline petered out and I needed sleep after the emotionally filled four days I had just experienced.

Jerry and I stayed at Daddy's. I heard the telephone ring and soon discovered no one was awake to answer the call.

I leaped out of bed and ran to the phone in the kitchen. My sister Marlene spoke.

"Wake up. You need to turn on the television set. The spacecraft Columbia started burning as it re-entered earth's atmosphere, and it is falling over Palestine and the Piney Woods in Texas." Marlene's a no-nonsense person, but I wanted a bit of nonsense at this hour of the morning. In the midst of the most joyous experience of my life, tragedy strikes.

"Call me back after you talk with your housekeeper. Make sure your home's okay." Definitely no-nonsense.

I cannot handle remotes for television sets. So I had to

wake up Jerry. I told him what Marlene said and he made it to the great room in two leaps, remote in his hand and television on in five seconds.

We saw video clips of the last moments of the Columbia's flight as it exploded and disintegrated over Texas and our trees. Dear God, what's fair about life? How can I reunite with my daughter and her family and experience such *joie de vivre* as other lives are snuffed out in the same moments in time? I sat in the great room and wept for the families of the Columbia crew and the unfairness of it all.

I need to add a comment about the Columbia debris around our home. Our housekeeper searched immediately for debris after I called her. She had heard the horrendous sound when the last of the Columbia soared over the house as it crashed onto the earth about 40 miles southeast of our home. And she found debris on our property over the next couple of days, calling authorities to come and get it. In the weeks following the disaster, the searchers walked our property and found many more pieces, including a 100 percent intact piece of tile from the Columbia. They allowed us to take pictures, and I will always remember my joyful reunion with Kate touched by the experience of pieces of the Columbia falling on our land. Tina worried for days about the safety of our home, and whether or not anything had fallen on it and caused damage.

We watched television for most of the day, trying to make sense from the confusion and chaos reported by local news stations. They often get on "live" to report something before they know the whole story. My favorite phrase, when I cannot change events occurring around me, is

"When I create my world, everyone will behave perfectly and everything will be perfect!" That phrase seemed to fit on that dark Saturday morning.

But by four o'clock, we were ready to have a party! We started arriving at Kate's on the hour. She had invited friends from the neighborhood and those with whom she shared our story. Family members got hugs, smiles, and love. As Kate's friends came, they knew immediately who I was. I do not know when I ever felt more loved and valued.

We ate and ate and ate. We played in the game room. Pool sharks challenged each other every hour. We talked on the patio and in the family room and in the kitchen. We took pictures for our family albums.

Life felt normal at this typical family gathering. This "new" normal felt good. Probably perfect.

Chapter 15

June 2003
Baby's Birthday

I celebrated Baby's birthday every year in my heart. One of her questions soon after we met focused on this: "Did you think about me on my birthday?"

"Yes!" I said.

Sometimes I went to an amusement park on her birthday to watch children play, imagining her doing something similar. Or I'd write a letter to her, and sometime in the years following, threw them all away. Oh, how I wish I had kept them to give to her.

So now that she was in my life again, I had to decide on a birthday gift for the first time. I didn't struggle much. I had a lot of family memorabilia and could make copies on the scanner. I decided to make a heritage family album with pictures and stories of her bio-family. I took pictures off the wall and scanned them. I took pictures out of photo albums and scanned them. I read family stories and printed parts of them in the album I composed for her. I wanted something lasting, something she could give Brad or Tina or their children, something to stand the traditional test of time.

And so I put it together on acid-free paper and all the

right stuff so that it will last 150 years. That's the guarantee.

I finished it and reviewed each page to ensure it looked just as I wanted. It needed more polish, but it looked authentic and told the story of my life. And that is what I wanted to give Kate. I wanted her to know from whence she came.

I sent it off to her to arrive on her birthday, and forgot Memorial Day preceded her birthday. It arrived the day after her birthday. The first chance I had to give her a birthday present, and it arrived late. Damn!

Chapter 16

July 2003
The Shaw-Bang!

When the plans began for the biennial Shaw Family Reunion, the cousins in Kate's generation scheduled it at our home in Texas. That announcement came when one of Jeannine's daughters married in 2001. Jerry and I gave our blessings on the location, which the family locked in place two years before the event.

Thirty-five members of the Shaw family had indicated they'd come for the big bash. We needed to have accommodations for each family and I felt gratitude toward local friends who spread the word about our event. Several friends called offering their spare bedrooms and we found space for each member of our family including a motor home offered by dear friends and discounted space in a local motel owned by other friends. I wanted Kate and her family to stay with us on their first visit. I needed a normal visit for my daughter's first time in our home.

Our celebration included our extended family reunion, my 60th birthday and the first time that *all* of the living biological descendents of my mother and father gathered in one place. What a celebration we planned!

We made photos a top priority after talking and eating! A local professional photographer agreed to come out and try to corral us for a family picture, and for any other single family units who wanted their family portraits done.

Some drove but most flew in because of the distances: New York City, Denver, Phoenix, Chicago, San Francisco and those in Iowa who never really left that beautiful spot on the planet. Kate and her family flew in from Phoenix and we planned to meet them in Houston.

She emailed me about a problem a few weeks before the event. Brad and Tina had given Kate a birthday gift, a French bulldog puppy, and she had to go pick it out. Since her birthday's only six weeks before mine, she got her puppy a few weeks before the reunion. So she and I had to determine what to do about Lulu Belle. Of course, I'm a sucker for animals and insisted she bring Lulu. And of course she brought Lulu, which meant buying another plane ticket on another airline, which came into another airfield in Houston, which meant traveling to two airfields to pick them up. Having a daughter's so incredibly fun!

We headed south to Houston early on the morning of July 16 in the 15-passenger van loaned to us by the church Jerry served. We made our first pickup, a lifelong friend from our days in Omaha, at Intercontinental Airport. She knew about Kate long before I broadcast my story to the world, the first non-family member I told, and she readily accepted our invitation to join the Shaw-Bang, 2003. With the change in plans, Kate and Lulu also flew into Intercontinental Airport in Houston, arriving just a short time after Ellie. It felt like a normal thing to do to go to the airport to pick up your daughter and her dog.

Next we headed to the second airport to get Brad and Tina and their dad. We traveled all the way across Houston, to the south side of the city. As I said, having a daughter is such fun!

The trio awaited us. The big van accommodated all of us and all the luggage very well. And then we did a normal thing, something families do. We drove home chattering and getting hungry and stopping to eat and driving again and then having to take a potty break and then driving again and finally we got home after the 13th, "How much longer?" All very normal. We drove down the road leading to our gate. And my eagerness built.

Early on I'd labeled our road the one the headless horseman rode in the Legend of Sleepy Hollow. The trees meet in an arch over the road. It's a dreamy and enchanting place at night, and just plain God-given gorgeous in daytime. My eagerness continued to build.

We drove down Sleepy Hollow Lane and turned onto our property. The lettering over the gate says, CONCORD LODGE. We'd lived here for six years, and now it's Kate's and her family's extended home. The tree house we built for Brad and Tina sits off to the right, and they spotted it immediately when we rounded the corner. We pulled onto the concrete driveway leading to the garage and piled out of the van. I felt about to explode with eagerness.

We could not corral Brad and Tina. They tore off to the treehouse and behaved like normal children.

We unloaded bags. Kate let Lulu out of the pet carrier and Lulu ran in circles, so happy for her release from confinement. Some family had already arrived and had dinner prepared. A kid-friendly dinner. Pizza! Lots of hugs and greetings and love shared again amongst family members. A normal thing.

But before we could eat, Kate came up to me and said, "Well?"

In all my attempts to convince myself of normalcy, I forgot that Kate had never visited the house before. She wanted a tour!

"I want to see the house! And I want you to show it to me!"

One tour does not cover everything at Concord Lodge. Here we display the memorabilia and artifacts from Jerry's and my individual and combined lives. Almost every item in the house bears a story. So I abbreviated the tour in order to accommodate pizza.

But we got to the family picture wall, and Kate and I spent several minutes there, identifying family members present and past. She looked carefully at each one. Some I'd put in her heritage album. Others she'd never seen before. I saw the emotional reaction in her face as she looked at pictures of people whose lineage she shared. People whose blood and genes and chemistry she now claimed. I could see in her eyes and feel in her spirit the reality of the experience.

C3   C3   C3

Shaw-Bang 2003 included an evening with friends of ours from town who always celebrate birthdays and special events together. They came out in droves that night, July 17, the anniversary of my mother's birth in 1916. I showcased my daughter at the event. The invitation read, *Kate's the Star!* I made it a take-off on her favorite champagne, White Star. But I also needed the world to know how proud I felt to claim her as my daughter. So incredibly proud!

We had cocktails and dinner on the deck by the pool on the hill behind the house. Everyone wanted to meet Kate. I made good on my promise to myself never again to feel shame at my experience of having given birth to Baby. That night I realized I conquered Shame and beat back Guilt. And Love, Hope, Redemption, and Forgiveness prevailed! I am alive and I have a daughter and I love her!

Several important events occurred that weekend. For the first time ever, all the biological descendants of my mom and dad, Merrill and Evelyn Shaw, gathered in one place. We took a family picture that included all of us, our spouses and loved ones. We valued this so because less than a year later one of our family fell to his death in a tragic accident on a roadside park near Buffalo, New York. We have a beautiful picture of him and his four-year-old daughter, Merrill May, named after her great-grandpa (Merrill) and her grandmother (Marlene May).

The second event was the opportunity for the Shaw family to open its arms to Kate and her family and, as Jeannine said, to let them slide naturally into the place that we kept for them. Well, they just slid into it and claimed it now and forever.

I marked every family gathering over the years by Kate's absence. I always felt her spirit and wanted to keep her place open for her return. And I feel pride in knowing that her cousins, aunts, uncles, grandpa, and the non-bio members of our family welcomed her with no question about her place in our lives.

Kate asked me as the weekend drew to a close, "Where is the nasty one? Isn't there someone here who isn't nice? Doesn't someone have a problem with me?"

"Everyone has done what he or she needed to do, and they all love you. So I guess you're just gonna have to deal with that!" I reassured her, knowing that I spoke the absolute truth.

I kept working on the new normal, a family that included a daughter and her family. I hoped that would never change.

Kate had the opportunity to reaffirm that with me. We sat on the deck and enjoyed conversation with several family members. Then I turned to her, struck again by the incredible newness of having her in our midst, and said, "Pinch me!"

Kate responded, "No! This is real and forever!" Forever. Deal with it. Normal. I think I can handle this.

೮   ೮   ೮

Gift-giving time occurs at every birthday party, even when the invitation says, "No Gifts Please." And that time came on the afternoon of my birthday, July 19. We sat on the deck talking and I began opening birthday cards that family had brought with them, and that friends had brought on *Kate's the Star* night. I began passing the cards around and Kate rose and said, "Oh, I'll go get your gifts."

I raised my voice. "Katherine, I told you, no gifts!"

Kate turned on her heel, whipped out her finger and pointed it at me, and said, "And when did YOU ever do what you were told?" And promptly marched off the deck to the applause and laughter of every family member.

I stood there in absolute shock. Shock that I have a daughter and she has done something normal like telling me that she's just like me and planned to do what she wanted when she wanted.

And she went into the house to get her gifts for me.

So the third miraculous experience of the weekend was her gifts. She had me open the first one because of its importance for my grandbabes. In Los Angeles, they walked into a shop displaying theme-accessories.

Brad spotted a theme-purse that had the name *Jo-Jo* on the side, and said, "Mom, that's Sharon's nickname. We have to get that purse!"

Kate agreed, and after having to find a second one because Brad spotted damage on the first one, and made the purchase. I will treasure this gift forever!

Kate's own hands made the second gift. I had told her the story of her birth. She knew I gave birth in a Catholic hospital attended by nuns who, in the 1960s, cared for their patients, but looked down on young women who had the audacity to get pregnant before marriage. Competent medically, my caretakers were grossly incompetent emotionally. In all fairness, I have no doubt today that this would happen in a Catholic hospital or anywhere else in the 1960s.

Family looking on as I opened the photo album
Kate had created for me.

I had told her that I'd asked the nuns for a picture of her. The nuns told me that wasn't possible. I did not tell her until later that I complained to the director of the adoption agency and, although I never got a picture of her, he did tell the nuns to allow me to have contact with her until I left the hospital.

Kate put her second gift in front of me. As I opened it, I realized it was a photo album. I opened the first page and saw Baby. The reality of her birth came flooding back. I remembered the 36 hours of labor, the rush to the delivery room where the on-call doctor announced, with no consultation with me, his plans to "push this along," and the final stages of labor slamming into my unsuspecting exhausted body. Tears began rolling down my face, tears of remembering, tears of regret, tears for all that I had lost, and tears of joy that we had all grown beyond that first experience, and that we'd celebrate the rest of our lives together. Startovers really do exist. Somehow the tears also marked all we had learned and accepted. My tears brimmed with love and joy.

The album contained pictures of her childhood, graduation from high school and college, marriage, and family pictures over the past decade. Kate shared her life with me in that album. I treasure it the most of any treasure in my home.

              ❧   ❧   ❧

Cousins and spouses in Kate's generation gathered on the deck late in the night of my birthday. Times like this usually turned rather funny, or, more accurately, hilarious. And sure enough, Karen, my niece, started one of her stand-up comedy routines. We rolled with laughter. I knew the entertainment was going to last longer than I could keep my eyes open, so I said good night to all and began to walk toward the house. Kate's husband called to me saying I needed to see another gift in the house. I rolled my eyes thinking, "This is getting embarrassing." He said I'd find it in my bedroom.

I couldn't see well in the dim lights of the bedroom. But as I approached the bed, I saw my beautiful granddaughter lying in bed, sound asleep. Tina gave me the best gift of all. I slept with my granddaughter for the first time in my life on my 60th birthday. I felt my immortality.

Totally spiritual.

ଔ   ଔ   ଔ

The last night of our weekend family event, after all extended family had departed, meant we could spread out into the motor home if we wanted. Brad decided that he wanted to do just that. He came tearing into the house—Brad seldom walks—and asked excitedly, "Can we sleep in the Bluebird? Huh? Please?" I cannot imagine ever saying no to him.

"Of course you can! Let's get your toothbrush and pjs and get you settled in there." I felt the contagion of his excitement and helped him and his sister move their stuff. Joel agreed to supervise, so he also made the move to the motor home. This marked his first solo encounter with his niece and nephew. Joel's report several weeks later suggested they told scary stories and had a marathon slumber party that night.

ଔ   ଔ   ଔ

The final gift that I received that weekend came from Christina, my soul-mate granddaughter. It occurred the last evening, after most of the extended family had left. We preserved Sunday afternoon and evening for just our immediate family. This is normal. Everyone else leaves, and just our family remains.

Late Sunday afternoon, Kate and I got together leftovers for a late afternoon snack. We chatted about the incredible weekend we had experienced, knowing we'd

95

travel to Houston on Monday to take them to their flights back to Phoenix. We'd take Kate and Lulu to one airport and Brad, Tina, and their dad to the other. Did I say what incredible fun it is to have a daughter?

As we chatted, Christina walked in and put her arms around me. I held her close. She said, "Can I ask you a question?"

"Of course, Sweetheart! Ask me anything you want."

"Would it be okay with you if I called you 'Gramma'?"

My heart stopped. Damn that heart-stopping thing. When will it ever end? My gaze jerked to Kate who mouthed a fast "Wow!"

I can't intrude. The child must lead. And this magnificent child led me. Then I saw a big smile on Kate's face that said, "Yes! This is good!"

And I said, "Yes, Sweetheart! You can call me anything you want. And if you want to call me Gramma, I'd love that!" And thus *Gramma Sharon* was born. Kate later reassured me Tina made the decision and she, Kate, supported it.

My next encounter with Brad that night included his calling me Gramma, so I strongly suspect the two colluded, and Tina won (or lost?) the toss about who asked me the question. After Gramma Sharon, of course Grampa Jerry was the obvious next step.

Afterword

January 2005

We just completed another awesome visit with our grandchildren. We find our experiences with them totally delightful. My favorite "Brad" story occurred as we played on the beach in San Diego shortly after the Shaw-Bang. We flew a box kite, running up and down the beach trying to keep it in the air. Since a little bit of running goes a long way, we talked them into having lunch and sitting for a while.

While waiting for our order, Brad suddenly turned to his dad and said, "Dad! Guess what! If you had been adopted, we'd have *four* sets of grandparents!"

Needless to say, we all dissolved into hysterical laughter. Nothing complicated about adoption for Brad!

They knew I wrote this story, and on a recent visit with them, they asked me if I'd read it to them. We spent several evenings just before bedtime reading parts of the book.

When we got to the part about Kate's first email, Tina exclaimed, "It came out of nowhere and mysteriously from someplace, Gramma. I wonder why my mom decided to send it to you then." This came from a very grown-up ten-year-old child!

I learned from Kate, and her best friend, Monique, that Moni's auto accident, in which she almost died, created the catalyst for Kate to contact the adoption agency and initiate contact with me. She knew she didn't want to wait too long and risk never knowing me because of her waiting. I also believe that as a result of my revelations to extended family in Iowa in January 2002, the energy of love that I felt, Kate felt. She felt safe contacting me. I no longer kept any secrets about her, and she'd be safe knowing me.

Kate and I talked numerous times about some strange coincidences in our reunion. Moni's accident occurred in the fall of 2001. Within six months I went to Iowa to tell my extended family about Baby. In the spring of 2002, Moni discovered the man she always called "Dad" was not her biological father. At his funeral, a family member told her the name of her biological father and offered her his telephone number. Kate supported Moni during this troubled time; on one occasion they drove in the car when Moni's cell phone rang, and it was her father.

After talking for a while, she handed the phone to Kate and said, "Here, talk to him!"

Kate remembered thinking, "I wonder how I'd feel talking with my biological mother."

She and Moni talked about Kate's response after the call ended.

Shortly thereafter, Kate Googled American Homefinding Association and entered the telephone number in her cell phone. It was on her phone list ready for the call she made in July 2002 telling Tom she wanted to contact me. She went shopping that morning in early July, and from that curious and thoughtful spirit of hers, said to herself, "I think I'll call AHFA!" She pulled off to the side of the road, scrolled down to the number, pushed the "call" button, and talked with Tom. And the wheels started turning that added the bonus to her life.

I feel so grateful she has such thoughtful and loving parents. We couldn't have reunited so easily if she'd led a different kind of life. Guilt on both our parts could have destroyed our relationship. But that did not happen. Thanks to her mom and dad, she led a healthy and complete life. I am her bonus. Her mom and dad are her parents.

In the third or fourth month of our reunion, I told Kate about her biological father. She had never asked about him, and I needed to tell her, in the event she also wanted to try to find him. She reacted with obvious distaste when I told her about his abandonment of me.

And then she said, "You know, I never thought about him. I only thought about you."

Just as I experienced with him, she felt only a minimal connection.

My comment, "Well kid, it's just you and me," after my final telephone conversation with him, somehow must have gone to her tiny senses even at that stage of her life.

ଔ   ଔ   ଔ

For 36 years, Tom said, "Timing is everything!"

Then Kate gave me a new mantra: "This is forever!"

I had times when I questioned the intrusion issue. I remain determined not to intrude into the life she had before she contacted me. She continues to reassure me that I will remain in her life forever. I have finally arrived, and I finally believe her.

As Kate says, "This is forever." When I go to sleep at night, I most often remind myself, this is forever.

And. . .I will always love you, Baby…always…

June 2005

About the Author

Sharon Shaw Elrod is a retired social worker and educator. She received degrees from three universities, BA in education from University of Northern Iowa, Masters Degree in Social Work from University of Nebraska, and EdD in Educational Leadership from Nova Southeastern University.

Her hobbies include music and gardening. Among her numerous volunteer causes are American Cancer Society, Anderson County Champions for Children and the Harvey Woman's Club. Shar and her husband live in the Piney Woods of East Texas on land that has been in Jerry's family since 1850.

Dearest Colleen —

This could have been "our" story too. Sher is my friend & has moved to AZ to be near her daughter & family — .

Lucky her!

I love you with all my heart & praise God for our relationship —

Mom
(maryelia)

Printed in the United States
37651LVS00001B/232-489

9 781932 196726